Boys WHO BECAME Prophets

Boys WHO BECAME Prophets

LYNDA CORY ROBISON

Illustrations by Paul Mann & Jerry Harston

Deseret Book Company

Salt Lake City, Utah

Library of Congress Cataloging-in-Publication Data

Robinson, Lynda Cory, 1946–
    Boys who became prophets / by Lynda Cory Robinson : illustrations by Paul Mann and Jerry Harston.
      p.   cm.
    Includes bibliographical references.
    Summary: Brief childhood biographies of fifteen prophets of The Church of Jesus Christ of Latter-day Saints, from Joseph Smith and Brigham Young to Howard W. Hunter and Gordon B. Hinckley.
    ISBN 1-57345-083-9
    1. Church of Jesus Christ of Latter-day Saints—Presidents—Biography—Juvenile literature. 2. Prophets (Mormon theology)—Biography—Juvenile literature. 3. Mormon Church—Presidents—Biography—Juvenile literature. [1. Mormons.] I. Mann, Paul, ill. II. Harston, Jerry, ill. III. Title.
BX8693.R625   1998
289.3'092'—dc21   98-37299
[B]   CIP
                                              AC

Printed in the United States of America   72076
Publishers Printing, Salt Lake City, UT

10   9   8   7

CONTENTS

Preface   vi

Joseph Smith   1

Brigham Young   9

John Taylor   17

Wilford Woodruff   21

Lorenzo Snow   29

Joseph F. Smith   35

Heber J. Grant   41

George Albert Smith   47

David O. McKay   51

Joseph Fielding Smith   57

Harold B. Lee   61

Spencer W. Kimball   65

Ezra Taft Benson   71

Howard W. Hunter   79

Gordon B. Hinckley   87

Bibliography   93

PREFACE

It was the first week in May, 1976, only three months since I had been called as a Targeteer B teacher (ages nine and ten) in the Midway (Utah) First Ward Primary, and I was discouraged. The children were tuning me out on the lessons about the prophets. A firm believer in allowing students to have their say, I asked how they would like me to make the lessons more meaningful to them.

"We want to know about the prophets when they were our age." "What did they do?" "What did they look like?" "Where do we girls fit in?"

With the help of a city librarian, I found some childhood stories of one of the prophets and experimented with them in class. The children loved them! Summer months gave me time to find more stories for the new group of children coming into class in September.

One girl's wondering response to the supplementary lesson materials was, "You mean Joseph Smith really had a mother?"

Unexpected surgery in the spring of 1977 took me out

of the classroom, and I was surprised at the greeting I received upon my return. The children had missed the childhood stories. The prophets had come alive and were real heroes to them!

It occurred to me that other teachers might appreciate this material; then I began feeling a strong impression that these stories were needed by the children themselves. As hungry as my students were, it seemed that the earlier the stories could be given to them, the better. As I studied ways to make them available, the idea of writing a book was born.

It has been a rewarding spiritual experience to work on this manuscript. I am grateful for the help of our Father in heaven in compiling these experiences.

I also wish to thank Gene Bryant, a former Sunday School student, who came up with the title for the book, and June and Harriett, who were the first to convince me to try doing it. Martha and Patricia always asked how I was doing, as did John, a former student, in his letters. My loving parents in Kansas never laughed at my awkward attempts, and their encouraging words helped when I needed them the most. Two Primary classes in the Midway First Ward critiqued the manuscript; Barton Clegg and Lisa Kohler especially gave helpful suggestions. I want to give special thanks to Don Norton, English professor at Brigham Young University, for editing help, and to Keith Perkins, BYU religion professor, for checking historical accuracy.

This book is dedicated to my son, Jason, and to many more future leaders in the Church.

J O S E P H
S M I T H

J oseph Smith, the boy from Vermont, did not like bullies. Once he passed a group of friends who had all been thrown to the ground by a bully. Joseph asked if he could join the fun. When the bully lunged at him, Joseph grabbed him by the collar and the seat of the pants, carried him to a ditch, and threw him in it. Then he helped the youth get up again, patted him on the back, and said he was sorry.

Another time when he was a young man, Joseph fought a man who had whipped his wife. Later in his life, Joseph said, "A man who whips his wife is a coward. . . . It was a hard contest; but I still remembered that he had whipped his wife, and this encouraged me, and I whipped him until he had enough."

Young Joseph Smith, who was born December 23, 1805, loved to have a good time. He played ball and had fun sliding on the ice. His favorite sport was wrestling, and he was very good at it. Joseph made many friends because of his cheerfulness and his tolerant attitude.

There were nine children in Joseph's family, and they

all loved each other very much. In the evenings the Smith family often sat around the fire together and told stories. Joseph and his older brother Hyrum were especially fond of each other. Whenever the two brothers had to be apart, for no matter how long, they would always greet each other with a hug when they met. This love lasted through their lives.

Father Smith taught his sons many things. He taught them to work hard in the fields with him. He taught them to love their country and their freedom. Many parents in the neighborhood had fought beside George Washington in the American Revolution. Being able to worship God as they chose meant a lot to these people, and Father Smith taught his sons to protect this right.

The Smith children did not go to school much, but the whole family knew the Bible very well because they had school in their home and read from the scriptures.

In addition to learning how to read, spell, and do arithmetic, the Smith children, as well as other children in the neighborhood, learned to do farm work and housework. By the time a boy and a girl were sixteen years old, they could take the father's or the mother's place in the home if they had to.

When Joseph was about seven years old, he had to have some diseased bone removed from his leg. He had suffered from a fever for three weeks, and his brother Hyrum often held his leg to ease the pain as he lay in bed. The doctor wanted to give Joseph brandy to stop the pain, and he wanted to tie him to the bed to keep him from moving during the operation. But Joseph said he did not want any liquor, and he asked his father to hold him in his arms tightly, so he would not move. His main concern was for his mother, who had often carried him in her arms to relieve his pain. She was so tired that he feared she could not stand to hear him cry, so he insisted that she leave the house. Only once did he scream out in pain.

The operation was a success. Joseph's leg was saved, though he walked with a slight limp the rest of his life.

We do not know much more about Joseph's childhood, because his mother wrote down only a few special events in his life. We do know that the family moved to Palmyra, New York, when Joseph was about ten. He later wrote that it was about this time that he began to think seriously about religion. He read about God in the Bible; he also spent many hours looking at the moon and the stars and thinking about the many beautiful animals, birds, and plants around him. He knew there must be a God; how else could all these marvelous things come about? "Only a fool could look at these things," he said, "and say there isn't a God."

Joseph Smith's parents taught all their children to love God. His mother often went to a grove of trees near their home and knelt in prayer. But Joseph and his family were confused, because none of the churches in their neighborhood seemed to teach the gospel the way it was taught in the Bible. Some members of the family joined one church, and some joined another church, because they could not agree on which church was best.

Joseph did not join any church, though he did attend some of the meetings in the neighborhood, and he listened to the preachers. He felt the same as many youth do today about religion. Joseph's own words were, "My mind was called up to serious reflection and great uneasiness;—my feelings were deep and often poignant." Still he did not join any church. Finally, when he was about fourteen years old, he decided he must know which church he should join. He also wanted the Lord to forgive him of his weaknesses.

One day when he was attending a religious revival (an outdoor church meeting), he heard a scripture that impressed him very much. Later, as he was reading the New Testament, he came upon that same scripture: James 1:5. It said that if anyone wanted an answer to a serious question, he should ask God, and God would

3

give an answer. Joseph decided to ask God for an answer to his question.

On a beautiful spring day in 1820, he went to the grove of trees near the farm and began to pray out loud. Suddenly a horrible feeling came over him, and he could not move his muscles. He later wrote in his diary that an "enemy of actual being from an unseen world" had attacked him.

He prayed harder. Just as he was about to give up, a beam of light came down through the trees, and the enemy left him. Joseph later told some of his friends that the light was so bright, he was afraid it would set the trees afire.

Then he saw two Personages in the light, dressed in white robes. One spoke to Joseph, calling him by name, and introduced the other person: "This is My Beloved Son. Hear Him!" These two visitors were God the Father and His Son, Jesus Christ.

At first, Joseph was so frightened that he could not speak. Finally he did ask his question about which church to join. Jesus told him not to join any of the churches, because none of them were completely right in their teachings. They had mixed the teachings of the Bible with the teachings of men and did not teach the complete truth. Jesus also said He was disappointed with the many people who "draw near to me with their lips, but their hearts are far from me." He meant that many people say they love Jesus, but only pretend to live their religion.

Jesus told Joseph Smith many other things, but Joseph was not permitted to repeat them or write them down. When Heavenly Father and His Son, Jesus Christ, left, Joseph was so weak that he could not get up. He lay still for a while, until his strength came back to him. Then he went home.

Joseph's family were the only ones who believed him when he told what he had seen and heard. When he tried to tell it to other people, they made fun of him. In fact, when Joseph's younger brother William was an old man, a reporter asked if he had ever doubted Joseph's story. William answered, "No, we all had the most implicit confidence in what he said. He was a truthful boy. Father and mother believed him; why should not the children? I suppose if he had told crooked stories about other things, we might have doubted his word about the plates, but Joseph was a truthful boy. That father and mother believed his report and suffered persecution for that belief shows that he was truthful. No, sir, we never doubted his word for a minute."

Even the local preacher made fun of Joseph and tried to get him to deny his story. Joseph's mother recorded that when Joseph was about fourteen, he turned into the yard to come home one evening, and an unknown person aimed a gun at him and fired. The bullet missed Joseph and hit a cow that was standing beside him.

Joseph knew that the Lord had a special mission for him. As he grew older, he began to wonder if his life was good enough for the Lord to still trust him with this mission. One night, when he was seventeen years old, he was kneeling in prayer at his bedside, feeling sorry for some of the things he had done.

While he prayed for forgiveness, the room began to fill with light. Then Joseph saw a messenger from God, standing in the middle of the light, just a few feet off the floor. This angel said that his name was Moroni. His message was that Joseph had a great work to do with a book of gold plates. After Moroni quoted many scriptures from the Bible, the light began to gather close to him, and then it took him right up to heaven.

As Joseph lay thinking about this marvelous visit, the room again filled with light, and Moroni returned. He repeated every word he had spoken during the first visit; then he explained what would happen at the end of the world. Finally he rose up into heaven again.

Later Moroni returned a third time, repeating all that he had said before. This time he warned Joseph that the

5

youth might be tempted to use the gold plates to get rich, but he must not do that, or the Lord would not let him have the plates.

These visits lasted all night long, and just as Moroni left the third time, Joseph heard the rooster crow. It was morning already.

The next day Joseph was so tired that he could not keep up with his father as they worked in the fields. His father was surprised, because Joseph was usually a good worker. He thought that his son must not be well. "Go home and get some sleep," he told Joseph.

As Joseph tried to cross a fence, he fell to the ground. A voice called to him. It was the angel Moroni again. Moroni repeated to Joseph everything he had said the night before. Then he commanded Joseph to go back to the field and tell his father everything that had happened. Joseph was afraid his father would not believe him, but the angel said that he would. And Joseph's father did believe him. Together they left the fields and went to the house to share Joseph's story with the rest of the family.

Later, Joseph walked to the hill where the angel had said the gold plates were hidden. He recognized instantly the exact spot where he should dig, because Moroni had shown it to him in a vision. He pried up a large stone, and underneath, in a stone box, were the gold plates.

As he tried to take them out, he felt a shock. When he looked up, there was Moroni, standing by him. The angel told him not to touch the plates yet. He told Joseph to come to this spot on the same day each year for the next four years. Then he would be permitted to take the gold plates from the hill.

Each year, when Joseph returned, Moroni met him and gave him instructions on what he was to do with the plates and how the Lord would help him do his great work.

On September 27, 1827, Moroni delivered the plates

to Joseph. He told the youth that if he ever did anything careless with the plates, the Lord would take them from him. If, on the other hand, he guarded the plates carefully and translated the writing on them into English, the Lord would protect him and the plates from any harm until the time came for Moroni to take them back.

As Joseph grew up, he learned many of the same things that other boys learned. But we can see that he had special qualities, too, qualities that helped prepare him to be the prophet who would restore the gospel.

With the help of the Lord, Joseph translated the characters on the gold plates. He learned of the wonderful church organization that the Lord would establish in our day. The scriptures that he translated were published in March 1830 as the Book of Mormon. A few days later, on April 6, 1830, The Church of Jesus Christ of Latter-day Saints was organized, with Joseph Smith as the first prophet, seer, and revelator of the Church. He served until his death in June 1844.

B R I G H A M
Y O U N G

One winter the Young family's supplies ran out. The father left for a three-day round-trip walk to town for more food. Brigham and his younger brother were left at home to continue clearing the land. They worked very hard, even while it was snowing. Using only hand tools, they worked all day to chop down a single tree. Then the tree had to be broken up and hauled away. When they went to the house, there was no food except some maple sugar, so they went to bed early to forget their hunger.

On the third day, as they walked to the house, Brigham saw a robin perched in a sumac bush. He hurried to get his father's musket, loaded it, and primed it with powder. Aiming it the way he had seen his father do, he pulled the trigger. The bird fell to the ground. The boys rushed into the house, tipped the flour barrel over, and pounded on the bottom of it. Two tablespoons of flour fell on the floor. They scooped the flour up, put it in a pan with the skinned and cleaned bird, added water, and made bird stew. They were so hungry, they ate every bite of it!

Brigham Young, like the Prophet Joseph Smith, was born in the state of Vermont, on June 1, 1801. When he was two years old, his family moved to Smyrna, New York.

The second daughter of the family, Fanny, was about thirteen years old when Brigham was born. Because their mother was sick with consumption, Fanny became the substitute mother for the family. Brigham would cling to her and cry if anyone else tried to hold him or take care of him. She carried him on her hip as she did the chores, even while she milked the cow. Strangely, the cow also refused to be taken care of by anyone else.

As a boy, Brigham was teased about making a path between his bed and the bread cupboard. Always having to go to bed hungry, he would get up for extra slices of bread and butter to snack on at night. In later years, after he was married and had a family of his own, Brigham made sure that the cupboards were full of crackers, fruit, and molasses so that his children need not be hungry between meals.

Brigham's family were very poor, but they were rich with love. After chores, the family would gather around their father and listen to him read stories from the Bible. Music was also important to them, and the children learned to sing solos and duets. There was very strict discipline in the home, for the father was a stern man. For example, he would not let his children listen to a fiddle, laugh, or shout on Sunday.

In Brigham Young's day, not many children who lived in the country went to school for very long. Few children learned to spell well. In fact, if a person could spell well and do simple arithmetic, he could become an elementary school teacher in a country school.

Although Brigham went to school only eleven and a half days in his whole life, he did learn to read. In fact, he became one of the most intelligent and well-read men of his day. He learned primarily from the things around him—his home, the forest, and the animals. He learned to make bread, wash dishes, milk cows, and make butter. He said later that he could "beat most women in house-keeping."

When he was probably not much older than six, Brigham watched the religious camp meetings in his area grow in size because so many people were looking for something spiritual in their lives. The camp meetings were loud, crowded, disorderly, and confusing. Preachers stood behind pulpits, all preaching at once, shouting to people passing on the streets. One preacher, Lorenzo Dow, converted Brigham's father and other family members to the Methodist Reformed Church, but he could not convert Brigham.

Brigham wrote in his journal: "He [Lorenzo Dow] stood up some of the time and he sat down some of the time; he was in this position and in that position, and talked two or three hours, and when he got through I asked myself 'What have you learned from Lorenzo Dow?' and my answer was, nothing but morals. He could tell the people they should not work on the Sabbath day; they should not lie, swear, steal, commit adultery, etc., but when he came to teaching the things of God, he was as dark as midnight."

Remember, Brigham was used to hearing his father read the Bible every evening after chores. He was taught by his family to be courteous and respectful by not ask-ing too many questions, but he watched plenty and thought plenty.

Once he overheard a minister's wife say to another woman in church, "Do you suppose that we shall be under the necessity of eating with our hired help when we get into heaven? We do not do it here, and I have an idea that there will be two tables in heaven." He saw supposedly good, honest men take advantage of their neighbors. About such persons he thought, "I did not

11

read the Bible as they read it. I wanted no religion that produced such morals."

Brigham's eleventh birthday started as a very sad day for him. As he did the dishes, he kept looking at the calendar, wondering why his mother had not remembered his birthday in a special way, as she always had in the past. Nobody in the family had even mentioned his birthday. It was hard for him to hold back the tears.

After finishing the dishes, Brigham and his little sister went to the garden to get some vegetables for supper. Brigham said, "Let's pick some rhubarb for tonight's dessert." His sister blurted out, "Oh, yes, it'll go nice with the ca—!" She put her hand over her mouth, but Brigham was too busy to notice.

That evening when the family came home from shopping in town, everyone was excited about a huge hat box they had brought. Once again, Brigham began to feel sorry for himself. He thought the excitement was over a new hat for one of his sisters. He went to his room. Seeing how sad he was, his mother followed him. She assured him that his birthday had not been forgotten at all.

After supper, the family ate a beautiful birthday cake. Then the hat box was brought to Brigham. Inside was a handsome new store-bought hat for him. Brigham asked if he might keep the hat in the box, and his mother agreed. As it turned out, that was the only hat Brigham ever had while he was growing up.

In those days families would spend all winter cleaning the trees and brush off their land so crops could be planted in the spring. When summer came, the family harvested the crops and sold what they did not need. The money from selling the crops would then be used to pay for the land. If the crop failed and there was no other way to pay for the land, it was taken away. The owner would then sell it again, but at a much higher price, because the land was already cleared.

Because of unpredictable crop failures, Brigham's

family had to move several times while he was growing up. The many years of hard work and family sorrows probably contributed to his mother's ill health. One day his father hurried to the fields to get Brigham, but his mother had died before they got back to the house. Brigham, who was only fourteen years old, went to his room and cried. Then he tried to remember all the things his mother had told him. Two things in particular stayed with him for the rest of his life: "Always honor the name of the Father and Son and reverence the Holy Book," and "Do everything that is good; help people in distress; and don't ever become angry, for if you do, you'll be overcome by evil."

After his mother died, Brigham left home. He had never worked for someone else, but he told the owner of a paint store that he would put in an honest day's work for his pay. The owner was so impressed that he hired Brigham. The young man's job was to mix paint. He soon invented a paint mixer that made the job faster, and this left him free to learn other skills. Over the years Brigham learned to be such a good carpenter, painter, joiner, and glazier that he was later able to go into business for himself.

As a young man, Brigham refused to partake of liquor. When other young men would say to him, "Take a glass," Brigham would reply, "No, thank you, it's not good for me." If the other young men insisted, "Why yes, it *is* good for you," Brigham's answer was, "Thank you, I think I know myself better than you know me." Brigham wrote in his journal, "And I have conceived from my youth that I could have my liberty and independence just as much in doing right as I could in doing wrong."

At age twenty-two Brigham joined the same church that his brothers belonged to, the Methodist Reformed Church, but he never was active in it. When he was about twenty-nine, he received a letter from his younger brother, Lorenzo Dow Young, telling about a dream Lorenzo had had. In this dream, Jesus was riding in a

13

white carriage with white horses pulling it. He stopped to ask Lorenzo about his family, then rode away. The dream bothered Lorenzo, and he decided to write Brigham about it. Brigham did not understand what the dream meant, but after careful thought, he decided to move to the same town where his brother and other family members lived.

Soon after he moved, Brigham heard about a new religion that had a book called the Book of Mormon. Members of the Young family obtained a copy of the book and read it. Brigham's father said that, besides the Bible, it was the greatest work and the freest of mistakes of any book that he had ever read. Several members of his family were baptized right away, but Brigham studied the religion carefully for two years. When he was firmly convinced in his own mind that he had found the true church, he was baptized.

Brigham recorded in his journal how he felt a difference in his life after he became a Latter-day Saint: "There was more or less of a gloom over my feelings from the earliest days of my childhood that I have in any recollection. Before I possessed the spirit of the Gospel [Mormonism], I was troubled with that which I heard others complain of, that is, with, at times, feeling cast down, gloomy and desponding, with everything wearing to me, at times, a dreary aspect. They appeared at times as though a veil was brooding over them, which cast a dark shade upon all things, like the shade of the valley of death, and I felt lonesome and bad." These feelings changed when he joined the Church, for then he had the Holy Spirit to guide and comfort him.

Brigham Young became a powerful leader of the Church. By 1835, three years after his baptism, he became an apostle. He was serving as president of the Council of the Twelve Apostles when Joseph Smith was killed in June 1844, and for the next three years the Council led the Church. Then, in December 1847, Brigham Young was sustained as president of the Church.

Brigham led the pioneers on their trek west. After the Saints were settled in the Salt Lake Valley, he sent families out to start new towns all over the area. He was responsible for over three hundred settlements, from Canada to Mexico, and from Colorado to California. He died in 1877.

JOHN

TAYLOR

Whenthe John Taylor, the third president of the Church, was a young boy, his best friend, Robert West, died from a serious illness. The boy's father, Allee West, moved from the village to become a shepherd, and John missed him very much. Feeling lonely for his friend's father, John asked one day if he could visit Allee. John's parents, knowing how close John had been to Allee, fixed a basket of food for him to take along.

It would take all day for him to get to Allee's house and back, so the ten-year-old boy left early in the morning. There were many hills to cross. Once, while resting, John was tempted to eat the food in the basket. He got up instead and walked the rest of the way as quickly as possible.

Allee was overjoyed to see John. They ate the food together and talked of old times.

Late that afternoon, some storm clouds began darkening the sky, so John left for home. Before he could get there, a thick fog settled on the hills, and he could not see very far. A team of horses almost ran over him because

17

the driver could not see the small boy walking on the roadside. When John came to a fork in the road, it was so dark and foggy that he couldn't see the landmarks that would tell him which way to turn. He fell to his knees in prayer. As he stood up, he felt a hand on his shoulder. It was Allee. He had worried about John's safety and had come to help his friend find his way home.

John was born in Milnthorpe, Westmoreland, England, on November 1, 1808. He was the second son in a family of ten. As a boy, John went to school, learned to plow and plant, and rode horses. He was a very spiritual boy, and he would often go into the fields to pray.

When he was eleven, his family moved to Hale, England, where they had inherited a small estate. It was the custom in those days to send the sons to learn a skill once they had reached a certain age. John was fourteen when he became an apprentice cooper, and the next year he learned to be a woodturner.

At age fifteen John became friends with a neighbor who had a drinking problem. He visited the man one day and told him what an example he had been in John's life. The neighbor, realizing how much he was hurting both himself and this young boy, promised to stop drinking.

In John's youth, he had a dream that puzzled him for some time. In the dream he saw an angel holding a trumpet to his mouth, sending out a message to the world.

The doctrines of the Methodist Church seemed more correct to John than the strict laws of the Church of England, so he became a Methodist when he was sixteen. One day he and a companion were walking to church when suddenly John stopped in the road and said, "I have a strong impression that I have to go to America to preach the gospel." This feeling was so strong that it stayed with him until he left England a few years later.

John's family moved to Toronto, Canada, in about 1830, and he joined them there two years later. In Canada he became a preacher for the Methodist Church. He met often with a group of fellow Methodists to study the Bible. During one of their many discussions on the Bible, they decided that the church they represented did not teach the same things as the Bible did. They made a list of principles they felt the true church of Christ should teach, including the following: (1) men should be called of God and ordained by proper authority; (2) there should be apostles and prophets; (3) the gift of the Holy Ghost should be given after baptism; and (4) there should be the gift of tongues, healing of the sick, and other miracles.

Members of John's study group fasted and prayed, asking the Lord to let them know if His church was on the earth. One day Parley P. Pratt, a missionary for The Church of Jesus Christ of Latter-day Saints, came to Toronto. John wrote down eight of Elder Pratt's sermons and compared them with the scriptures. He rejoiced to find all of the sermons in agreement with the teachings of the Bible. Soon he and other members of his group became baptized members of the true church of Jesus Christ.

John Taylor was ordained an apostle in 1836, two years after his baptism. He was with the Prophet Joseph Smith in Carthage Jail when the Prophet was murdered, and he tried to knock down the mob's guns with a cane. He was wounded severely, but his pocket watch stopped a bullet from entering his chest.

Because of John Taylor's fine education, he wrote many pamphlets, articles, and books for the Church. He became the third president of the Church in 1880, three years after the death of Brigham Young. The Primary organization was started under his presidency. He died in 1887.

WILFORD

WOODRUFF

What boy can resist a good fishing hole? Certainly not Wilford Woodruff and his brother. This stream was full of spotted trout, and it also fed their father's mill! When they had free time during their work for their father, the boys dropped hooks into the water below. They gained the reputation of being the most successful fishermen in the village. Wilford enjoyed fishing, hunting, and sports throughout his life.

Wilford Woodruff was born March 1, 1807, in Farmington, Connecticut. Tragedy struck his family while he was yet an infant; his mother died from spotted fever when he was only fifteen months old. Somehow he sensed the loss of his mother and sobbed at her death. Wilford's father dreamed the rest of his life about his son's sobbing. Shortly after Wilford's mother died, his father married again, so Wilford was reared by a loving stepmother.

The school was two miles from the Woodruff home. Wilford later wrote, "In those days parents did not feel the importance of urging upon their children the advantage of education as they urge them today." Thus, Wilford worked on his father's farm, as most of the boys did in his day, and went to school for only a few months during the coldest part of the winter, when the farm work slowed down.

Wilford's father had a large farm with many cattle, a flour mill, a sawmill, and a carding machine. Because of his father's generous nature in trying to help other people meet their financial obligations, the family farm was lost. The hardships the family faced made a strong impression on Wilford. All his life he made it a practice to avoid debt, and he was extremely careful to make his word good in all business matters.

Young Wilford was always a hard-working boy. His chore at age six was to feed the cows and the bull. He was particularly fond of one cow, calling it *his* cow. One day when he fed the cows some pumpkins, the bull stole his cow's pumpkin. This made Wilford so angry that he reached over and got the pumpkin the bull had left, planning to give it back to the cow. The bull charged, and Wilford ran down the hill. His father yelled, "Drop the pumpkin!" But Wilford was too scared to let it go. Suddenly he tripped, and the pumpkin rolled out of his hands and ahead of him. The bull leaped over Wilford and ripped open the pumpkin with its great horns.

Wilford had many accidents in his life. When he was three years old, he fell into a kettle of boiling water and almost died. It was nine months before he was well again. Another time he was severely hurt when he fell from the top of the barn to the floor, right on his face. These two accidents and some others happened because he had disobeyed his parents.

At age six Wilford made a decision that is recorded in his journal: "One Saturday evening, with my brothers Azmon and Thompson, while playing in the chamber of my father's house, contrary to his instructions, I made a misstep and fell to the bottom of the stairs, breaking one of my arms in the fall. I suffered intensely, but soon

22

recovered, feeling that whatever I suffered in the future, it would not be for disobedience to parents. The Lord has commanded children to obey their parents; and Paul says, 'This is the first commandment with promise!'"

So seriously did Wilford consider this decision that he went to his father and apologized for not obeying by dropping the pumpkin when the bull was chasing him. His father only laughed and said he was surprised that Wilford even heard him while trying to get away from the charging bull.

However, in spite of his efforts to avoid them, the accidents still happened. In his journal Wilford wrote, "Evidently, I have been numbered with those who are apparently the marked victims of misfortune. It has seemed to me at times as though some invisible power were watching my footsteps in search of an opportunity to destroy my life. I, therefore, ascribe my preservation on earth to the watchcare of a merciful Providence, whose hand has been stretched out to rescue me from death when I was in the presence of the most threatening dangers."

By the time he was twenty years old, Wilford had broken his leg in a fall from a carriage, had been kicked in the stomach by an ox, had been buried alive when a hay wagon overturned on top of him, and had narrowly escaped when a horse pulling a wagon he was in bolted down a hill. Once he might have died when caught in a blizzard, but he was saved by a neighbor. Another time he fell fifteen feet from a tree limb and landed flat on his back. Other times he nearly drowned in thirty feet of water, split open the instep of his left foot when chopping wood with an ax, and was bitten by a dog that had rabies.

When Wilford was seventeen, a bad-tempered horse he was riding threw him on a rocky hill. Fortunately, he landed on his feet in a standing position; landing in any other position would have killed him. Still, he broke both ankles, and one leg was broken in two other places as well. This happened at two o'clock in the afternoon, and by the time the doctor came at ten o'clock that night, Wilford had lost consciousness.

As an adult, he had yet more accidents. Twice he fell from the top of a mill wheel but escaped being crushed to death. Twice he was dragged by runaway horses, and once a gun aimed at his chest misfired. One day a falling tree hit him in the chest, breaking his breastbone and three ribs and badly bruising his left thigh, hip, and arm.

When Wilford Woodruff was eight years old, the Baptist Church started a strong religious revival in the area where he lived. Baptist ministers preached in his father's home. Wilford attended the meetings, prayed, and tried to feel religious, but he could not.

When Wilford was fourteen, the Presbyterians began another religious revival in Wilford's town. He wrote in his journal the difficulty he had in accepting their religion: "I attended the meetings, inquiry, Sunday Schools, and prayer meetings. I tried to get religion by effort and prayer, but my efforts created darkness instead of light and I was not happy in the attempt. They wanted us to give our hearts to God without telling us what to do or explaining any principle in a comprehensive manner. There were many young people at that time of my age who made a profession of religion. I did not wish to make a mockery of sacred things by professing light when I had received none, so I kept aloof from all professions."

During the family's struggle to provide for all their needs, Wilford and his brothers spent the summers living first with one family and then another, to earn money. Wilford had been working this way for a couple of summers when, at age sixteen, he had his first real attack of homesickness. The man he was working for was very stern and did not talk to Wilford except to ask or answer questions. Wilford wrote, "I ate and slept very little for two weeks. Relief, however, came to me when I started to school and made the acquaintance of my

24

fellow students. My homesickness left me and never came back."

Wilford left home when he was twenty years old. For three years he worked at his Aunt Helen's flour mill, where he became an excellent miller. During his free time he read the Bible. "The Lord is very near me here," he said, and he often felt so close to the Lord that he thought he could reach out and touch Him. He prayed constantly for the light of truth.

Wilford and his brother Azmon bought a farm near Richland, New York. While they were out in the fields one day, two Mormon missionaries came to the house and talked to Azmon's wife. As Wilford was coming in from the field, he felt a strange surge of joy. When Azmon's wife told him of the missionaries, Wilford left without eating supper to attend their meeting at the schoolhouse.

Wilford knew instantly that what the missionaries said was true. He recognized the truth partly because of an elderly friend, Robert Mason, who had taught him as a child that the church of Christ was not on the earth at that time, but that it would be restored during Wilford's lifetime. He also believed the missionaries because of what he had read in the Bible.

He wrote in his journal, "At an early age my mind began to be exercised upon religious subjects. I did not then join any church for the reason that I could not find a body of people, denomination, or church that had for its doctrine, faith, and practiced those principles, ordinances, and gifts which constituted the gospel of Jesus Christ as taught by Him and His apostles. I learned also from the Scriptures that—the God of heaven would set up His Kingdom; that an angel would restore the gospel; and that it would be preached in all the world for a witness before the Savior should come to reign."

Wilford was baptized a member of The Church of Jesus Christ of Latter-day Saints on a very cold, wintry day in December 1833. The snow was three feet deep and the water was mixed with ice and snow, but Wilford said he never felt the cold!

Wilford Woodruff was ordained an apostle in 1839. He kept very accurate journals, and was called as one of the early historians of the Church. He served many successful missions and was able to baptize about 1,800 people in England. He kept in touch with every one of these people, writing each one a letter at least once a year!

Wilford Woodruff was sustained as president of the Church in 1889. He died in 1897.

L O R E N Z O
S N O W

Lorenzo Snow, the fifth president of the Church, was also the fifth child in his family. He was born April 3, 1814, in Mantua, Ohio. The wild frontier had had a lot of timber to clear, and there were only about ten families in the area. The nearest market for their crops was New Orleans, which took six months round-trip to reach. Wheat sold for forty cents a bushel, and beef sold for a dollar fifty per hundred pounds. Eggs were four cents a dozen and chickens five cents each.

Members of the Snow family were known far and wide for their honesty. They were Baptists, and they regularly read the scriptures and had family prayers. The parents did not allow the children to attend dancing school or participate in the theater, but they kept an open mind on religion. They were willing to discuss doctrines with many people from different churches, and they had many friends.

Lorenzo was a faithful and obedient child. His sister recorded in her journal that even when he was small,

29

Lorenzo was orderly and precise in all things. His ambition to always do his best brought him success in everything he did. He especially loved reading; when he was not doing chores, he was usually reading a book.

One day his father asked Lorenzo to check one of their fields to see if it was ready to be plowed. When he went to grab his hat, he found that his coat, which he had torn, had been repaired. His mother told him that his sister Eliza had fixed it for him as a surprise. This touched Lorenzo very much.

Because of the many things Eliza did for him to show her affection, Lorenzo and his sister became very close. Their love for each other lasted all their lives. They felt that they could talk about anything with each other.

The Snows' ten-acre field was only a short distance from the house, enclosed by a tightly woven willow fence. When Lorenzo picked up some dirt to see if the ground was dry enough to plow, he heard a noise from the bushes. Looking up, he saw a huge bull. The frightened boy searched for an escape. A white oak tree stood ahead, and Lorenzo got to it just as the bull crashed through the fence.

It was cold sitting in that tree with the bull pawing the ground underneath him and slashing the air with its long horns. The wind went through Lorenzo in spite of his coat. He kept looking to the house to see if help was coming. With his teeth chattering and his hands numb, he prayed: "Dear Heavenly Father, thank you for all your blessings. And please, dear Lord, tell my father to come and help me." Just then his father came riding on his white horse, carrying a big bullwhip. The bull hated the whip. One angry crack and the bull let out a mad roar, then went running until he was out of sight. Lorenzo's father climbed the tree and got Lorenzo down, half-frozen and scared to death.

When Lorenzo was a small boy he saw an army drilling and a military band playing. He decided then that he wanted to be a soldier when he grew up. His sister Eliza sewed him a military uniform, which thrilled Lorenzo. But he felt that he needed more education to become a successful soldier. All his life he had worked hard. He had been able to go to school only during the three winter months each year, because he was needed at home. So he sold some property he had inherited and went to a Presbyterian college in Oberlin, Ohio. Soon he wrote home: "If there is nothing better than is to be found here in Oberlin College, good bye to all religions."

During his travels to college Lorenzo had met David W. Patten, an apostle of The Church of Jesus Christ of Latter-day Saints. They talked about the church and religion. Impressed that Brother Patten was indeed a man of God, Lorenzo never forgot him. Then letters from home announced that his mother and one sister had been baptized into the Mormon Church.

Four years later, just before Lorenzo left college, he got a letter from Eliza. She wrote that she too had just been baptized a Latter-day Saint, and that she had moved to Kirtland, Ohio. She was teaching school at the Prophet Joseph Smith's home. Knowing that Lorenzo had a desire to learn Hebrew, she invited him to Kirtland to study it with a well-known scholar there. Lorenzo decided to go to Kirtland. While there, he met the Prophet Joseph Smith. After much study, prayer, and conversation with other members of the Church, he gained a testimony and was baptized.

As a member of The Church of Jesus Christ of Latter-day Saints, Lorenzo served as a missionary, then settled in Nauvoo, Illinois. When he and his family were driven from Nauvoo with the Saints, he was called to preside over the Saints at Mount Pisgah, Iowa. Without food and clothing, and with many persons seriously ill, the Saints were in a desperate situation. Elder Snow organized the men into groups. Some went to nearby towns to find work so that they could buy food and clothing. Other men repaired wagons or made items to sell, such as chairs, tables, and butter churns. Some were sent to Ohio

31

to ask for contributions from rich men not of the Mormon Church, and they collected $600. Lorenzo also organized games, socials, parties, and plays to keep the people in good physical, mental, and spiritual health. Finally, without any serious accidents, the company made it across the plains to the Salt Lake Valley.

Lorenzo Snow was ordained an apostle in 1849, a year after his arrival in the Salt Lake Valley. He helped to settle and build up Brigham City, sixty miles north of Salt Lake City, with many types of industry.

When President Wilford Woodruff died, Lorenzo Snow went to the Salt Lake Temple to pray. As he was leaving the Celestial Room, he saw and talked with the Savior, Jesus Christ.

Lorenzo Snow was sustained as president of the Church in 1898. At that time the Church was in great financial trouble, and President Snow traveled many hundreds of miles to meet with the Saints and urge them to pay their tithing. When they responded, the Church prospered and was able to pay its debts. He died October 10, 1901.

JOSEPH F.
SMITH

Joseph F. Smith, a nephew of the Prophet Joseph Smith, was born November 13, 1838, in Far West, Missouri. His father, Hyrum, named him after the Prophet because Hyrum and his brother loved each other so dearly.

Just two weeks before Joseph F.'s birth, his father was unjustly put in jail, accused of doing things he had not done. After Joseph's birth, his mother, Mary Fielding Smith, was ill for several months. Hyrum Smith first saw his son when Mary made a bed on a wagon and had friends drive her and the baby to Liberty Jail, where Hyrum was being held.

Later, when Mary went again to see her husband in jail, she left baby Joseph home with an aunt. A mob came to the house and looted it, turning a mattress over on top of the baby and nearly suffocating him.

Soon after Hyrum was released from the jail, the family moved to Nauvoo, Illinois.

In Nauvoo Mary was in charge of a committee to raise funds to buy nails and glass for the temple.

Sometimes she would keep the money in a drawer at home before turning it over to the committee. One day five-year-old Joseph found this money in his father's desk. He put some of it into his pocket to listen to it jingle; then off he went to play. One of the neighbors asked him about the money in his pocket and took him home to his mother, saying that Joseph had "stolen the money from its secret hiding place." Joseph was innocent, but the sound of being called a thief stayed with him all his life. He never again wanted to hear the word being used about him.

Until he was six, milk was about the only food he had, because his family was so poor. The lack of more nourishing food made him look very pale. One day, when the Prophet Joseph was visiting, he put the boy on his knee and talked to him. After a while the Prophet asked Hyrum why the boy was so pale, and then counseled him to feed the boy a little more solid food, even if there was not very much available. The Prophet's concern so touched young Joseph that he never forgot it.

When Joseph was six years old, his father reached down from his horse and picked up the boy to kiss him good-bye. That was the last time Joseph ever saw his father. Hyrum, with the Prophet Joseph, was murdered by a mob at the Carthage Jail. Late at night a neighbor gently tapped on the window and said, "Sister Smith, your husband has been killed." Even as a grown man, Joseph could still remember the screams of his mother when she heard the sad news.

Joseph remembered his father well all his life. The favorite hymns he sang as a grown man were the ones his father had taught him as a little boy.

When Mary Fielding Smith and her family were forced to leave their home in Nauvoo, they decided to head west with the other Saints. Joseph, though he was only eight years old, drove one of the ox teams. The wagon-train master did not want the Smith family to come because they were without a father to do most of the heavy work on the trail, but Mary insisted that they could get along without any help from others. In fact, she said her wagon would get to the Salt Lake Valley first, just to prove they could do it.

Mary Fielding Smith had many spiritual experiences on the trip west, some involving Joseph. Her model of faith and her ability to get answers to prayers left an unforgettable impression on him.

Once the family's oxen wandered off, and no one could find them. When Joseph came back into camp hungry and tired from searching, he saw his mother kneeling in prayer. She then got up confidently and went in the opposite direction from where the oxen were last seen, even though the men yelled that she was going the wrong way and wasting her time. Joseph followed her, and within minutes she beckoned. The oxen were caught in some trees below the riverbank, completely hidden from view.

While the family was camped at Winter Quarters, Nebraska, Joseph's job was to herd cattle. One day he and three companions took the herd of cattle from the pioneer towns out to pasture. Suddenly a gang of Indians came over the hill. One of the boys ran for help, but Joseph knew that if the cattle were lost, the Saints would have to spend another winter in Nebraska before heading west. A skilled horseman, he quickly rode his horse toward the herd and yelled until the cattle began to stampede. Two of the Indians rode up beside him, lifted him off his horse by his elbows and legs, threw him to the ground, and took his horse. Just then some men came over the hill, shouting and waving pitchforks. So the Indians quickly left with no cattle—but they did have Joseph's horse.

In September 1848 the wagon train reached the mountains east of the Salt Lake Valley and camped for the night. The next morning when they woke up, they discovered that the Smith family's cattle had wandered off and could not be found. The wagonmaster refused to wait until the oxen were found, and he ordered the other wagons to continue over the mountains. When they were halfway up the mountainside, a storm came up suddenly. The wagonmaster ordered everyone to unhitch their teams and to put rocks behind the wheels so the wagons could not roll back down the mountain.

In the meantime, Mary and Joseph had found their cattle and hitched them to their wagon just as the storm ended. Then they headed up the mountain. Soon they passed the other pioneers, whose oxen were scattered in the storm. Joseph's uncle asked Mary if they shouldn't wait. She replied, "They have not waited for us, and I see no necessity for us to wait for them." They forged ahead, and they actually did arrive in the Salt Lake Valley first!

Joseph was ten when they reached the valley. The family built a small cabin in which to do their cooking while they slept that first winter in the wagons. After two years of hard work, they were able to build a comfortable home and obtain some land.

They paid their tithing with the finest animals and crops—the tenth pig, the tenth chicken, the tenth egg, the tenth load of potatoes, and so forth. A clerk at the tithing office once made fun of Mary Fielding Smith for paying tithing when she was a widow and had so little. This made her very angry. She was proud that the Church records showed she never needed any help from the Church—she always did her share and more.

Thus, Joseph F. Smith gained a testimony at an early age of the importance of keeping all of Heavenly Father's commandments. His mother set an example even when others who should have known better made fun of her. This gave her and her family strength to take care of daily problems.

Mary died when Joseph was thirteen. Because of all they had been through together, Joseph felt a great loss at her death. When he was fifteen he was called to serve a mission in Hawaii. Within months after he arrived in the mission field, he had learned the language and earned the love of the people. He was called to be the mission leader for the islands when he was sixteen, and he served until he was eighteen.

Joseph F. Smith was ordained an apostle in 1866, at the age of twenty-seven. He was also named as a counselor in the First Presidency. He became the sixth president of the Church in 1901, and set an example in everything he asked the Saints to do. He encouraged Church members to study, practice love and kindness, and gain a testimony. He died in 1918.

H E B E R J.
G R A N T

Heber J. Grant was born November 22, 1856, in Salt Lake City; he was the first Church president born in Utah. His father, Jedediah M. Grant, was a counselor to Brigham Young and the mayor of Salt Lake City; he died when Heber was only nine days old. Years later, Heber wrote in his journal, "Although my father died when I was a babe nine days old, years later after his death I was reaping the benefits of his honesty and faithful labors."

Heber's mother did her best to meet the family's expenses by sewing for other people and having renters in her home. Heber slept in a large ventilated closet so that his room could be used for renters. At that time, flour was often too expensive to buy in Utah, and butter was an unknown luxury. There were times when the family had only four pounds of sugar for a year's supply. One Christmas Heber saw his mother cry because she did not have enough money to buy even one stick of candy for him.

When the struggles became too much, the family had

to sell their home. The money they received, five hundred dollars, was divided among the Grant heirs. With her share of the money, Heber's mother bought a small adobe home. The day they moved, Heber sat down on the front lawn of the lovely old home and cried. Then he shook his fist and said, "When I'm a man, I'll buy you back."

Once during a heavy rainstorm, Heber and his mother had to set at least six buckets on the floor of their little house to catch the rain leaking through the roof. The bishop offered to build a new roof with fast-offering money, but Heber's mother refused. She told him that she could get along until her son grew to manhood and could build her a new house. Within a few years Heber did build a new house, and he asked the bishop to dedicate it. Because of his memory of his mother's struggles, Heber tried to help widows and orphans financially throughout his life.

Heber and his mother were very close. She used to say that she would take care of him when he was growing, and later he could take care of her. "So near the Lord would she get in her prayers, that they were a wonderful source of inspiration to me from childhood to manhood," he once said.

Sister Grant had a great deal of faith in her son. She taught him that he could succeed in the business world and become a leader in the Church. One of his aunts also predicted that Heber would be a high Church leader. And once, at a dinner party in the home of Heber C. Kimball, a counselor to President Brigham Young, Brother Kimball picked up young Heber, sat him on the table, and prophesied in the name of the Lord that he would be an apostle and be a greater man in the Church than his own father. Heber's mother constantly urged him to behave so that this prophecy would come true.

Heber was invited to attend the U.S. Naval Academy, but instead he stayed home to take care of his widowed mother. He became a very successful businessman. In his spare time he read all he could to improve his mind. His habit was to mark in a book the things that impressed him most and then pass the book on to a friend.

His natural desire to excel in everything prompted Heber to learn many skills in life that he might not otherwise have learned. When other boys made fun of his clumsy baseball playing, he shined the renters' boots at five cents a pair until he had saved a dollar to buy a baseball. He pitched the ball hour after hour on a barn wall. He was called "the laziest boy" in the neighborhood because he spent so much time throwing the ball, but he made the team that won the territory championship.

His handwriting was also very poor when he was a schoolboy. However, with practice, he later earned a diploma for the finest penmanship in the Territory of Utah.

He couldn't hear musical notes well, but a friend said anyone who had a good voice and would practice could learn to sing. Within a few months Heber had learned six songs.

When Heber was nine years old, his aunt and cousin came to Salt Lake City for general conference. Heber and his mother went back to St. George with them and stayed six months; the trip took thirteen days by wagon. While in St. George, Heber went to school in a tent.

Once Heber was a water boy in the third-floor gallery of the Salt Lake Theater. He used a five-gallon coal-oil can as a water bucket, which he filled from a well across the road from the theater. He so hated to miss the show that many times he wished the "gods of the galleries" would fill up on water before they came to the theater. He also had a small acting part in the play *Uncle Tom's Cabin*.

In one of the schools Heber attended in Salt Lake City, the students were to go upstairs to a quiet room for part of their classwork. An older boy with a stick was the monitor who made sure everyone was quiet. One day Heber noticed a boy going into the room with a slate, pencil, and sponge. The boy dipped the sponge into a pot of hot water on the stove and squeezed the boiling water onto Heber's chair. Heber did not sit down, of course; but he returned the favor and did the same to the other boy's chair. The monitor caught Heber and was going to punish him, but he found out the truth in time.

Heber wanted revenge for almost getting whipped by the monitor. He had heard that if you tell a person often enough that he looks sick, that person will soon believe it. So Heber and a few of his friends told the boy for five days, "You really look sick. You should see yourself in the looking-glass." The boy finally went home, feeling really sick, and Heber felt better.

One of Heber's treasured prizes from school was an award from the teacher—a piece of paper four inches long and an inch and a half wide, with the word "TRUTHFUL" printed in blue ink.

Every spring Heber enjoyed playing marbles. His favorite game was Knuckle-down-Boston. The boys would draw a large ring in the dirt with a stick; they put their marbles in the middle and rested their knuckles on the outer line. Each player would take a turn shooting at the marbles, and when they played "keeps," the winner got to keep all the marbles he knocked out of the ring. Heber's pockets were always bulging. His favorite competitor was Injun Charlie, an Indian boy adopted by a neighbor. Heber and Injun Charlie played with the other boys, but they were so good that when they played with each other, a large crowd would often gather to watch them.

It was about this time that people began to see Heber's ability to succeed in business, for he used his marble winnings to hire other boys to go home and do his chores for him. Some of the neighbors believed his mother had hired the boys because her own son was too lazy to do the chores.

While playing marbles one day, one of the boys pointed out a well-dressed man walking down the street.

The man was a bookkeeper for the Wells Fargo Bank, and he made a salary of one hundred and fifty dollars a month—a lot of money in those days. Heber made up his mind right then that he was going to be a bookkeeper so he too could earn that much money. At age fifteen he became a bookkeeper and errand boy for an insurance office.

Heber J. Grant was just twenty-five years old when he was ordained an apostle in 1882. He was sustained as the seventh president of the Church in 1918 and served for twenty-seven years. During this time, the Church welfare program was started and three new temples—in Hawaii, Canada, and Arizona—were dedicated. President Grant died in 1945.

GEORGE

ALBERT

SMITH

The young man took an egg from his grandmother's chicken coop to trade for a piece of candy at the store. The clerk gave him the candy, and George Albert Smith reached up carefully to give him the egg. As the clerk took it, the egg exploded, and the clerk and all the customers ran out the door. George hadn't known it, but the egg was old and rotten!

George Albert Smith, a distant cousin of the Prophet Joseph Smith, was born in Salt Lake City on April 4, 1870. One of fifteen children, he was taught early to work hard and be self-supporting. His parents and home life were described as ideal by neighbors and friends. Family members were loving and affectionate, and religion and honesty were taught and lived in the home. George loved being outdoors; he especially enjoyed swimming with the other boys in the Jordan River and herding cows.

When George was twelve, he was sent to live with relatives in Provo so that he could attend Brigham Young Academy, which was then holding classes in an old warehouse. Karl G. Maeser was George's favorite teacher. "Not only will you be held accountable for what you do, but also for the thoughts you think," Brother Maeser taught his students.

George's father was called on a mission for the Church when George was thirteen. George went to work at the ZCMI clothing factory, sewing buttons on overalls for two dollars and fifty cents a week. He used this money to help the family while his father was gone.

The Smith family home had clay-like dirt around it, and no grass. Depending on the weather, there was either ankle-deep dust or sticky mud. When George was thirteen—working at ZCMI, milking cows, cutting wood, carrying the coal and water—he often wished there was grass and a shade tree that his friends could sit under when they came to visit. He and his mother made it a family project to have a lawn before George's father came home from his mission. They planted the grass and soon it was coming up. Then a thunderstorm washed out months of work in one afternoon. The only money available for more grass seed was the extra money George had earned doing small jobs at school during the winter. He had planned to use this money to buy a much-needed new suit. For two days he wrestled with the decision; then he decided to spend his extra money for more grass seed. This time the grass grew, and the lawn turned out to be a very nice surprise for his father.

George's patriarchal blessing, which he received at age fourteen, promised him that if he remained true and faithful to the gospel, he would be called to be a "mighty prophet."

That year George asked Mr. Webber at ZCMI to hire him again. Mr. Webber offered a job he did not think George would take—driving a team of horses and feeding and currying them for one of the traveling salesmen. George accepted the job. He took pride in all he did. On the way home from a selling trip to Southern Utah, he cleaned the wagon in Provo; then, a little further on, he cleaned the horses. Mr. Webber praised him, saying no one had ever brought the team back as clean as George had.

The next day Mr. Webber asked George to make cardboard boxes. George was determined to make more boxes than the other workers, who usually made about sixty each day. The first day he made one hundred!

The manager then assigned him to work as a wholesale grocery salesman, and he soon became manager of all grocery sales for ZCMI in Salt Lake City. By age twenty he had become a successful traveling salesman. For relaxation during his selling trips, he played the guitar or harmonica while his traveling companion played the flute.

Once George borrowed money from the bank and staked almost everything he owned on helping a man who was an alcoholic. The bank disapproved, and it was a long time before the man showed that George Albert Smith's trust was well placed. But the man did overcome his problem, and later he became a great leader in the Church.

George Albert Smith was ordained an apostle in 1903. He was active in Scouting all his life, and received the Silver Buffalo and Silver Beaver awards.

In 1945 he was sustained as the eighth president of the Church. Harry S Truman was the president of the United States at that time, and President Smith offered him the Church's aid for people in countries that had suffered greatly from World War II. When President Truman asked how soon the food, clothing, and other supplies could be shipped, President Smith answered, "It's all ready."

President Smith was noted for his great love of his fellowman. He died in April 1951.

DAVID O.
McKAY

David O. McKay, the ninth president of the Church, was born September 8, 1873, in the small town of Huntsville, a few miles east of Ogden, Utah. While growing up on his family's farm, David had a dog, a pony, pigeons, rabbits, and a magpie that he taught to talk.

When he was seven years old, David had his first deep sorrow in life. His two older sisters became very ill. The older one had rheumatic fever and died; the younger sister caught pneumonia and died on the day of her sister's funeral. So the family dug the older sister's grave bigger and buried both sisters together, side by side.

Soon after this, David's father was called on a mission to Scotland. David's mother was expecting her sixth child. The family had just made the last payment on their farm and were hoping to add a new room to the house. A mission meant that those plans would have to wait, but David's parents knew that they must do as the Lord wished. A baby girl was born just ten days after David's

51

father left for his mission, but news of his daughter's birth did not reach him until he was in Scotland.

David was told that he must "take care of Mama" while his father was gone, and he worked hard. A man was hired to take care of the cattle and do the heavy outside work. He brought with him a team of oxen, and they became a burden on the family at times.

Soon after he arrived at the McKay home, the hired hand left to visit relatives. Young David had to feed the oxen as well as the other farm animals, and the oxen never seemed to get full. With tears in his eyes, he told his mother, "Give them two armfuls of hay and then let's run to the house before they eat it."

The neighbors helped the family harvest the crops. On the advice of a neighbor, David's mother stored their grain until the following spring, when the prices were better. The family made such a good profit on that crop, and also on the next season's grain, that they were able to build the addition onto the house after all. When David's father came home, he was surprised to see his growing baby daughter and a bigger house, too!

David's father was called to be a bishop. Since there were no hotels or restaurants in Huntsville, the McKay home was often opened to overnight guests. The dining-room table was always set up on weekends for visitors who came through town. Young David met lots of people this way, including many of the General Authorities of the Church.

John Smith, the Patriarch to the Church, came to the McKay home many times. When David was fourteen, he received a patriarchal blessing from Elder Smith. After pronouncing the blessing, the Patriarch looked into David's eyes and said, "My boy, you have something to do besides playing marbles."

David went into the kitchen where his mother was preparing dinner and told her, "If he thinks I'm going to quit playing marbles, he's mistaken." His wise mother stopped working and tried to explain to him what Elder

Smith had really meant, though even she did not fully realize the full meaning at that time.

Sometimes David's father had to attend Sunday morning church meetings in a small town five miles north of Huntsville, and he and David would ride the big white horse together. While his father attended the meetings, David would ride the horse home to attend Sunday School in his own ward. One day the blanket slipped off the horse, taking David with it. The horse was too big for David to climb back up, so he walked all the way, carrying the blanket and leading the horse. It didn't occur to him to disturb the bishop's meeting to get his father to help him.

David loved to swim, ride horseback, read books, play baseball, dance, sing in the glee club, and serve in the Church.

Though he was too young to play on the local baseball team, he was occasionally asked to substitute when one of the players injured himself. Once when David was at bat, the umpire called "strike two," and the pitcher disagreed with the call, saying it was strike three. When David did not move, the pitcher rushed toward him, yelling, "Get out of here, kid, or I'll crack that bat on your head." A hush fell over the crowd, but David was calm. "The umpire called only two strikes," he said. "Go back to the pitcher's mound and try to get me out. You have one more chance."

Seeing the determined look on the young boy's face, the pitcher went back to the mound and pitched a swift, straight ball. David got a two-base hit. The next player hit a single, allowing David to run to home plate and win the game. Everyone cheered for David. They were proud he had stood up to the bully when he knew he was right.

As a teenager, David delivered newspapers between Huntsville and a small town on the other side of the mountain. He would leave early in the morning, ride on his horse all day, and come home in the evening. He even made his deliveries in stormy weather, because he knew his customers were expecting their papers. During the long stretches of horseback riding, he tried not to waste any time. He read books and memorized poems, learning material that he later used in his speeches as a General Authority.

Years later, David talked often about how his father had handled the farm chores. Each morning at the breakfast table, David's father would ask, "Boys, what is your plan for today?" Then David and his brothers decided on the most important jobs needing to be done. Because the father continued asking this same question even after David and the others were adults, the children felt the farm belonged to the whole family instead of just to their parents.

David O. McKay became a schoolteacher and then a principal when he was a young man. He was called as an apostle in 1906. He became the ninth president of the Church in 1951, and traveled all over the world sharing the gospel. He often stressed the importance of having love in the home. He encouraged the Saints to hold family home evenings, and urged parents to love their children and children to love their parents. He died in January 1970.

JOSEPH
FIELDING
SMITH

Young Joseph Fielding Smith had a horse named Junie. He insisted that she was a very intelligent animal. It didn't matter how many times Joseph locked the barn, Junie could always undo the strap on the stall door with her nose and teeth. When she got out, she would turn on the tap water in the yard. She never ran away; she just waited for the noise to arouse Joseph so he could turn off the water and put her back in the barn.

One day Joseph's father teased him about Junie being smarter than her master. He showed the boy how to buckle the strap around the post and under the crossbar. Then he said to the horse, "Young lady, let's see you get out now." Joseph and his father left the barn and walked across the yard, but before they had reached the house, Junie was at their side. Joseph grinned and said, "Father, now who's smarter?"

Joseph Fielding Smith was born July 19, 1876, in Salt Lake City. Joseph F. Smith, his father, was the sixth president of the Church. He was often away from home because of his responsibilities in the Church and community. He also had to leave home at times to avoid angry enemies of the Church who sought to put him in jail.

One day Joseph was waiting in the parlor for a special blessing from his father when he saw his mother getting ready to leave with his father and his baby sister. Young Joseph was used to his father's leaving, but his mother had usually not gone also. They were going to Hawaii, a long way from home, and Joseph was afraid he would never see them again. He was eight years old and had just been baptized, so he felt he must be brave and not cry, but he could not help himself. Tears were in his parents' eyes, too. Joseph stayed with his older brothers and sisters while his parents were away. He was very happy when they returned two and a half years later, bringing a new baby brother with them.

The Smiths had a farm in Taylorsville, Utah, where Joseph did farm and household chores. He irrigated and helped harvest the hay and took care of the livestock. One day while he and his brothers were herding the cows, they felt hungry. They bought a loaf of bread from a neighbor, but when they sliced it, they found it full of flies. They quickly lost their appetites.

Twice Joseph hurt himself while haying. The first time, he and his brothers wanted to save themselves a trip to the hayfields by putting an extra load of hay on the wagon. That was to be their "tithing load." As they drove into the yard of the tithing office, a bar across the top of the gate caught Joseph and knocked him to the ground, breaking his leg.

Another time Joseph and his brother George were bringing in the hay and stopped to let the horses have some water at a canal. Then Joseph asked George to hold the horses' bridles while he climbed up and took the reins. George either did not obey or did not hear him, and walked behind the wagon. Something scared the horses and they bolted, throwing Joseph off the hay and between the animals. Joseph felt sure it was the end of him, but somehow he managed to get himself clear of both horses and wagon.

One day Joseph decided to milk the cow secretly by himself just to prove he could do it. He did it so well that the job of milking the cow was his from that time on.

Joseph was very close to his mother. She taught him about prayer and about Joseph Smith and the Prophet's vision. During the summertime when his chores were done, he enjoyed sitting under a tree reading and memorizing the scriptures, because he knew them to be true. He loved to read the history of the Church and any other books he could get hold of to read.

Joseph Fielding Smith became very knowledgeable about Church history and doctrine. He served as the Church Historian for nearly fifty years. Saints around the world enjoy his more than twenty-five published books.

In 1910 Joseph Fielding Smith was ordained an apostle by his father, Joseph F. Smith. He became the tenth president of the Church in January 1970. During his presidency he helped in genealogical work by opening temples in Ogden and Provo, Utah, and obtaining microfilm and records from many countries. He died in July 1972.

HAROLD B.
LEE

Harold B. Lee was born March 28, 1899, in Clifton, Idaho, one of six children. The family lived on a farm, and Harold had chores to do from the time he was a small boy. The chores had to be done shortly after daybreak each morning so the men could start the day's work when the sun came up. There were also evening chores, and sometimes they had to be done by the light of a lantern.

When he was older, Harold would have to work all summer to help pay his way through school in the winter, and even then, he usually had a part-time job in the winter.

The family had cows for milk, butter, and cheese, and there was always enough wheat in their storage to make flour and cereals. They also had chickens, a vegetable garden, and fruit trees and bushes.

Harold's mother was a good seamstress. When the older children grew out of their clothes, she would alter them for use by the younger members of the family. They rarely had "store-bought" clothes. When Harold was four years old and his brother Perry was six, she made them suits trimmed with lace and ruffles. As soon as the boys were out of sight of their parents, they would tuck the lace and ruffles under so their friends would not make fun of them.

Harold had long curly hair as a child, and his mother enjoyed combing it into ringlets that hung below his shoulders. This embarrassed him and caused other children to tease him and laugh at him. Finally, one day he took the scissors and chopped off the curls. His mother cried while his father finished cutting the hair to even it up.

The Lee family loved the gospel. They learned to listen always to the promptings of the Spirit. Several times this helped save Harold's life.

One day Harold was standing in front of an open door watching a heavy storm. The lightning and thunder seemed to be very close. Suddenly his mother gave him a push that knocked him to the floor. At the same instant a bolt of lightning flashed down the chimney, across the room, and out the open doorway. Had Harold still been standing there, the lightning might have killed him.

Harold was just a small boy when he had his first personal experience with listening and obeying the voice of the Spirit. One day he was playing outside while his father was busy doing farm work. Harold saw some old buildings on the other side of the neighbor's fence and decided to go play there. He pretended the buildings were old castles to explore. As he started to climb over the fence, he heard very distinctly a voice saying, "Harold, don't go over there." Thinking the voice was his father's, he looked around, but he saw no one. Then he realized that he was being warned of unseen danger, so he returned to his own yard.

When Harold was eight years old, his mother sent him to the pantry one day to get a can of lye so she could make soap. The shelf was high, and the can slipped out of his hands and spilled all over him. His mother quickly grabbed Harold so that he would not run, kicked a lid off a large vat of pickled beets, and poured cup after cup of the red vinegar juice all over him. This neutralized the lye so it would not burn him.

When Harold was seventeen, he had pneumonia. His mother used a mustard plaster on him, but that did not work. Then she sliced a panful of onions and put them in an empty flour sack. The wet, juicy sack lay on his chest while she prayed. The next morning the crisis was over, and he was breathing well again.

When Harold was in his teens, he cut an artery on a broken bottle in the fields. His mother was able to stop the bleeding, but the wound later became infected. She burned a clean black stocking to ashes, opened the wound, and rubbed the ashes into it very carefully. The wound healed quickly.

One night Harold's mother asked his father to go find him. She felt that something was wrong, and she was right. Harold's horse had thrown him into the stream. He was bruised and wet, but unhurt.

Harold decided to be a schoolteacher. He studied hard and passed an examination in fifteen subjects when he was just seventeen years old. That year he was appointed principal of the Silver Star School near Weston, Idaho, a few miles from his home. He was the only teacher in the little one-room school, as well as the custodian and groundskeeper. He taught school for nearly four years and then served a mission.

Harold B. Lee was ordained an apostle in 1941. He became the eleventh president of the Church in July 1972. Under his direction, the first branch of the Church in Jerusalem was opened, and stakes were organized for the first time in Chile, Korea, and the Philippines. The Mutual Improvement Association was placed under the direction of the priesthood, and several programs about the Church appeared on television. President Lee served for seventeen months as Church president, until his death December 26, 1973.

SPENCER W.

KIMBALL

Spencer W. Kimball was born in Salt Lake City on March 28, 1895. When he was just three years old, his father was called to be the stake president in Thatcher, Arizona. So Spencer grew up on a farm in Arizona. While the family cleared their ten acres of stumps, young Spencer would find a stick, tie it to a makeshift wagon, and ride it all over the trails in the cornfields behind the house.

Other children made fun of his middle name, Woolley, a family name that he himself disliked. He also disliked it if anyone called him Spence instead of Spencer.

Though the family was poor, the children were not aware of it. It was common in the small farming town to have hand-me-down clothes, homemade shirts, and patched pants. Even if food was scarce, the family found some way to laugh about it.

Arizona is a very dry desert area, and the people there trusted to God for rain and sunshine for the crops. Once all the members of the stake fasted for rain for two

Sundays in a row. Another week passed, and finally the rains came.

Spencer learned very early how important the Church and the gospel are. The family always sat on the fourth row of the chapel for Sunday School and sacrament meeting. They knelt in prayer before each meal, with the chairs turned away from the table and plates turned upside down. Evening prayers were said at their mother's knee, and sometimes for family prayers the family members knelt around the revolving piano stool, putting their hands together, one over the other. When they all were touching one another, they felt very close.

One day, when Spencer was five years old, his one-year-old sister got lost. After the mother and children prayed, Spencer's older brother got up and went straight to her. She was sound asleep in a large box behind the chicken coop.

The Kimballs' best hay grew in the west fields, and Spencer's father always had the boys load the wagon with that hay for the tithing barn. One summer Spencer and his sister planted a patch of potatoes. In late summer they dug the potatoes and cleaned them, then dressed themselves in clean clothes and went off with the potatoes in their little wagon. They sold the potatoes for about two dollars, which they planned to spend for candy, ice cream, and Christmas presents. Then their father gently reminded them of tithing. "The Lord has been kind to us. We planted and cultivated and harvested, but the earth is the Lord's. He sent the moisture and the sunshine. One-tenth we always give back to the Lord for his part." Spencer and his sister felt honored and privileged to pay their tithing.

Spencer's first experience with miracles happened when he was six years old. Leo Cluff, a three-year-old neighbor boy, had been gored in the side by a cow. The doctor cleaned Leo's wounds and sewed the boy up. As Leo's skin began changing color, the doctor said he wouldn't survive because of the infection. The Cluff family asked Spencer's father to give Leo a priesthood blessing. The next day the doctor waited in town for the Cluff family to come and make funeral arrangements. When they did not come, he got in his buggy and went out to their home. There was Leo, awake and getting better.

When Spencer was baptized on his eighth birthday, he overheard someone say he looked older than eight— "like a chubby little bishop." His brothers teased him about that for a long time.

Most children began school at age six, but Spencer's mother felt that children should begin school at seven, so that was when Spencer started the first grade. He was never absent and never tardy.

In the second grade Spencer would usually spend his lunch hour running the three blocks from school to home. He would water the cows and horses, feed the pigs, eat his lunch, and then run back to school without being late. One day he went home in the middle of the morning and started the chores. He had goofed. It was not noon, but recess time!

Spencer ran back to school, face red, to face the children laughing at him. Terribly embarrassed, he broke into tears, and the teacher could not get him to stop. Finally she announced that Spencer was way ahead of his group; he was to move up a grade with the children his own age. That pleased him, and he stopped crying.

Spencer was a giggler, and many times his teacher had to put him on the dunce seat to settle him down. One day he and a girl across the room, Agnes, broke into giggles and could not stop. The teacher moved Spencer over to sit by Agnes, but this made them giggle even more. Finally Spencer had to sit by the teacher's desk in front of the room. He became serious very quickly.

Spencer was described as a "boy's boy." Everyone liked him. He made people laugh and have a good time; he was always good-natured and friendly and seldom quarreled. He could outwrestle anyone his own size, and he got lots of scoldings from his sisters and mother for his dirty knuckles and torn overalls. Once he almost drowned on a family outing. Though he later learned to swim, he remained afraid of deep water.

The children had to work long hours on the farm, and sometimes Spencer fell asleep at the supper table. To lessen the boredom of tedious work, he would memorize the ABCs, the times tables, or the Articles of Faith. While milking the cow, he would squirt milk in the mouth of the cat, or memorize word-perfect the Ten Commandments to the beat of the milk squirting in the bucket.

The buggy always had to be washed, greased, and painted; fences had to be whitewashed; the trellis must be kept painted green; and the barn, granary, and harness shed had to be painted. Spencer's job was to feed the pigs. He joked many years later that carrying so many five-gallon buckets of slop to the pigs had stunted his growth.

When he was ten, Spencer learned to work with his father on important letters. His father would dictate letters on Church business, politics, and personal matters to Spencer, who wrote them in longhand and then typed them with his two-finger method.

At his father's request, Spencer started to take piano lessons. He lost interest after the first two weeks, but when his father promised he could practice the piano instead of working in the fields, he became interested again. He learned to play well.

Spencer's mother died when he was eleven. He had been very close to her, and he missed her greatly. The house seemed empty to him, and he found himself crying while milking the cows, feeding the animals, and at night after he went to bed. He had been used to running home after school and calling out, "Ma! Ma!" She would answer and ask what was wanted, and he would run back out the door, saying, "Nothing." He loved her more than anybody else in the world. He tried to be like his father, but he always felt he had been paid the nicest compliment when anyone said he reminded them of his mother.

As a deacon, Spencer was playful, but he took his duties seriously. If his companion did not show up when they were to collect fast offerings, he would go out to do it himself. When he was fourteen the Sunday School superintendent met him after class one Sunday. Spencer was afraid that he was going to be scolded for teasing the girls and pulling their hair. Instead, he was asked to teach a Sunday School class. The next year he was called to be the stake Sunday School chorister.

One day at stake conference one of the speakers, who was a daughter of Brigham Young, asked if everyone had read completely through the Bible. After conference Spencer went home, got out the Bible, and began reading. It took about a year to finish reading it, and he did not understand some parts of it, but he felt good knowing that he had kept a promise to himself.

Spencer W. Kimball became a successful businessman in Arizona before he was called as an apostle in 1943. He became the twelfth president of the Church in December 1973. During his presidency, he stressed the importance of missionary work and urged the Saints to "lengthen their stride." Several countries, including Communist Poland and Nigeria, were opened to the missionaries.

Under President Kimball's direction, there were changes in the genealogical program and in the Church meeting schedules. Several revelations were added to the scriptures, as well as an official declaration extending the priesthood to all worthy male members.

BENSON

Can you picture a bald Scoutmaster? That's what happened to Ezra Taft Benson when he was nineteen. He had promised his Scout troop a hike to Bear Lake if they worked hard to win the regional choir contest. The boys won! One of the Scouts wanted all of them to have short hair so they would not need combs or brushes on their outing. The town barber joked with Ezra. He offered free haircuts to the whole troop if Ezra would let him shave his head. So, one bald Scoutmaster and one bald Assistant Scoutmaster took the troop to Bear Lake to fish, camp, and swim! Since then, President Benson has been active in Scouting because "the youth are our future." He has received national awards from the Boy Scouts of America for his work and interest in this worldwide organization.

Ezra came from an ideal family in an ideal community. Whitney, Idaho, was Ezra's hometown. It was a close-knit community of 300 people. Most of them were related to one another.

His parents adored each other and enjoyed laughter

71

and singing. They created a warm, fun atmosphere with their dry humor and teasing, and were happiest when the family was all together.

Ezra's father had strong country loyalty and loved the soil. He was a leader among the valley farmers in agricultural knowledge. (The word *agriculture* means the "science of farming.") He was well known for running things perfectly and smoothly—an efficiency expert.

Ezra's mother was a very detailed, organized homemaker and an outstanding cook. She took an advanced sewing class and was able to clothe her family at a very low cost. Ezra had six brothers and four sisters, so all of these homemaking skills helped his mother take good care of them.

During the crop harvests men and boys worked side by side in the fields, while women and girls worked side by side baking bread and pies. Every year there were parades that ended in the whole town singing patriotic songs. Afterwards, they all ate picnics of fried chicken, salads, hot dogs, and ice cream on their family quilts before riding on the Ferris wheel.

Church parties were plentiful. The participants skied behind a horse, skated, and bobsleighed. There were picnics on the town baseball diamond after a good game. Entire families danced with each other at the church while babies slept on a pile of blankets.

At Christmas and Thanksgiving the Benson family took turns going to the two sets of grandparents' houses. Arriving in a sleigh with bells on their horses, they could expect singing and dancing in both homes.

Ezra Taft Benson owed his very life to both his grandmothers. When he was born on August 4, 1899, the doctor did not think he would live. The doctor took care of Ezra's mother while both grandmothers dipped Ezra in cold water, then in hot water, then back into cold water and so forth until he began to breathe.

"T" was one of Ezra's nicknames. One day "T" sat in his high chair. His mother had been teaching him good manners by saying, "How do you do?" to their guests. "T" looked down at the table, and in his best toddler voice he began to politely greet the food. He began with, "How do you do, eggs?"

It was the family tradition to have dad as the hero. When Ezra's father said "no," he meant no the first time. He also taught his children to treat their mother's requests with the same respect. Ezra's father did not allow quarrels while he was in the house. It was all right to tease each other as long as there was harmony and love that went with it.

Ezra wanted to learn everything he could from his father at an early age. He became an apprentice farm-hand at the age of four, and by the age of five, Ezra could drive a team of horses. At age seven he thinned sugar beets, herded cattle, tended chickens, hunted eggs out-side the hen house, dug potatoes, and milked cows. There were no machines or electricity to help him with these chores.

Ezra learned a valuable lesson in high school one day. During a test he asked a student in the next row if he could borrow a knife to sharpen his broken pencil. The teacher picked up Ezra's test because it looked like he had been cheating. Then the teacher told Ezra that he wouldn't be allowed to play in the school basketball game that night. But Ezra's father, the coach, and the principal believed Ezra was telling the truth because he was always honest. Right before the game started, they decided he could play. Ezra was upset by this experience and chose to "avoid all appearances of evil" after that.

The high school was far enough away that he would ride his pony to and from school. On the way he would set muskrat traps and then check them on his way home. The money he made from selling the pelts to a Chicago furrier paid for books and clothes for school. He gave the leftover money to his parents.

At age sixteen Ezra thinned one acre of a neighbor's beets in one day, which set the record. Ezra had lots of job offers because of his accomplishment. He learned all about seeds and how to make better farms from his father, who let him send for farm magazines to keep up on the latest farming research. He watched the farmers in Whitney gather all their crops after harvest to make one big crop. This type of cooperation helped them sell their crops at good prices. It was easier for a buyer to purchase one big crop than a whole bunch of little crops. Ezra's love for scientific farming later played an important part in his life.

Ezra's father made sure his family never went hungry. He always had a year's supply of food and fuel. He also knew farm life was hard if there was no fun to go with it. After several days working in the beets, the whole family went to Bear Lake to fish and swim for a couple of days. During cattle round-ups, his father would take the family up in the canyons to camp out.

Each Saturday's chores were done by one o'clock sharp. The family would then spend the rest of the day in fun activities. In fact their farm became a place for the youth of the community to meet for fun. There were horse races, foot races, baseball, rodeos, swimming, hiking, picnics, bobsleighing, skiing, and skating. His dad even made a basketball court by rolling and packing the dirt down solid and putting up a basket at both ends of the court. The Bensons had the first record player in Whitney for dancing and listening to music. But, Ezra's most favorite activity was shooting a game of marbles. One year he started out with only ten marbles and ended up with over a thousand because he had won so many times.

In April 1915, the home evening program was written about in the newspaper. The Prophet Joseph F. Smith promised those members who held home evening that "great blessings will result. Love at home and obedience to parents will increase. . . . The youth of Israel . . . will gain power to combat the vile influences and temptations which beset them." Because the Bensons had a strong testimony of the gospel, Ezra's father told his family, "The Presidency has spoken, and this is the word of the Lord to us." They had their first home evening that very night. Each week the children would take turns praying, conducting, teaching lessons, planning a program, making refreshments, singing, reading scriptures, telling pioneer stories, writing letters to relatives and missionaries, playing games, or sharing their talents.

Going to church was an accepted part of the Bensons' lives, one they never doubted. A sister always baked a cake Saturday morning. Clothes were laid out on Saturday night. Ezra's father felt that the Spirit of the Lord was present when church meetings began and insisted on being punctual. Sometimes one or two tardy children had to run to catch up with the buggy as it left the house on time. A sick horse made them late once, but they still arrived during the opening hymn. Ezra's mother taught him about the temple each time she ironed their temple clothes. Prayers were always offered kneeling around the table morning and evening and before leaving to do the farm work.

When Ezra harnessed the horse and buggy for his mom to make the rounds as Relief Society president, he would put one-half bushel of wheat into the buggy. The Church welfare program was not in effect yet, so the Relief Society sisters would keep the wheat and take it around to others in need. Thirty years later, as an apostle, Ezra took wheat and supplies to European Saints after World War II.

Ezra was twelve when his father was called on a mission. He and his father had become best friends, and Ezra missed him very much. He worried that he would never see his father again, but his sweet mother comforted him. Ezra and his mother had a special bond and gave strength to each other while his father was gone. His mother had raised the other ten children to look up to Ezra because she felt there was "something distinctive" about her oldest son. He loved his mother dearly, and to him she could do no wrong.

Missionary letters from Ezra's father were full of the Spirit, and this was felt in the Benson home. Family prayers were given so intensely by his mother that the children thought twice about doing something that might go wrong. With father not at home to read the scriptures, Ezra read the Book of Mormon by himself. He had already followed his father's example by accepting the gospel and living its teachings many years before his father left on his mission. Even though Ezra was known for pulling pranks, this early testimony of the gospel and being busy on the farm kept him out of trouble.

It was no surprise that Ezra also wanted to go on a mission. He memorized his father's letters with delight. Family commitment to the gospel was strengthened even more after his dad's mission. When his father returned, Ezra sang hymns so many times during chores that he soon knew them by heart. Once, he heard his father praying for a political candidate during an election year. When his father's candidate lost the election, he heard his father praying for the man who had won.

At age sixteen Ezra went to get his patriarchal blessing. He came home very happy. One of the promises made by the Lord was that Ezra would go on a mission if he continued to live worthily. This promise was fulfilled when he served a mission in Great Britain.

Ezra studied agriculture and vocational training in high school because "a man ought to be able to repair something." He returned to Whitney after college with two academic degrees in agriculture and became the county farm agent. He visited each farmer and brought them together to help each other. As he was promoted during the following years, he did the same thing on the county, state and national government levels. This type of cooperation did not go unnoticed. In 1952, the president of the United States, Dwight D. Eisenhower, asked him to be his secretary of agriculture in Washington, D.C.

"Mr. Secretary," as Ezra was called, was the expert on farm issues, and he met farmers all over the country to see what they needed. National leaders asked him for advice on farm problems because they could depend on Ezra to live his religion and to be truthful. Years later he stated, "It pays to live the standards of the Church and be true to the faith."

In November 1985, Ezra Taft Benson was called by the Lord to be the thirteenth president of The Church of Jesus Christ of Latter-day Saints. During his presidency, more temples were built, genealogy records became much more computerized, and missionary work increased. Temples and missions were started in eastern Europe after important events in our world history: the Berlin Wall was torn down, we fought for Kuwait's freedom in the Persian Gulf war, and the Soviet Union underwent many political changes.

President Benson's counsel to the Saints was to read the Book of Mormon and use its teachings, love their fellowmen, live the gospel with confidence, and prepare themselves to face any future events. On his ninetieth birthday, 4 August 1989, he wrote, "I do not know fully why God has preserved my life to this age, but I do know this: That for the present hour He has revealed to me the absolute need for us to move the Book of Mormon forward now in a marvelous manner."

HUNTER

There they were, the neighbor-hood bullies at the irrigation ditch. Seven-year-old Howard stopped to watch them. What were they doing with that cloth sack? They kept throwing it in the water and laughing. Finally the boys threw the sack on the ground and walked away. Howard opened it and found a tiny kitten inside. He hurried home and showed it to his mother.

When she told Howard that the kitten was close to death, he replied, "But Mother, we have to try." So she found a box, and they lined it with a blanket and put the kitten on the blanket. Then they slid the box under the coal stove in the kitchen. The warmth of the stove dried out and revived the poor little animal. To Howard's delight, the kitten soon recovered, and it lived with the family for many years.

Howard W. Hunter was born on November 14, 1906, in Boise, Idaho. He was the first prophet to be born in the twentieth century. Two years later his sister, Dorothy, was born.

One day soon after Dorothy was born, Howard was running in the house and tripped. He put out his left hand to try to catch himself and tipped over a pan of very hot water that his mother had just taken off the stove and placed on the floor to cool. Howard's hand and arm were badly burned. The doctor told Howard's mother to pack his hand and arm in mashed potatoes and then wrap the wound with strips of cloth for a bandage. The burn healed, but he had the scar for the rest of his life.

When Howard was nearly three years old, his parents built a new home. His father bought a small hammer for his son, and Howard enjoyed helping his father pound nails for the living room floor. The house was heated by a coal stove in the living room, and there was a coal stove for cooking in the kitchen. Howard's father ran a pipe from an outside well into the kitchen sink to provide running water.

The small home had just one bedroom, where Howard's parents slept. He and Dorothy slept on the front porch, which had canvas screens to keep out the snow in the winter and the sun in the summer. There was plenty of room on their large lot for a vegetable garden and pens for Howard's pets. His favorite rabbits were named Bunny Boo and Mary Jane, and his constant companion was his dog, Daisy.

When Howard was four, he and Dorothy went with their mother on the train to Utah to visit relatives. While they were there, Howard became sick and had to stay in bed for a week. His father wrote a letter to his mother and told her that Howard's friend Buster was also sick. When the family got home, Howard's mother found out that both Howard and Buster had been stricken with polio. Buster was crippled for life, but the disease only affected Howard's back. It was stiff the rest of his life, and he was never able to bend forward and touch the floor.

The next summer Howard went to visit his aunt and

uncle on their ranch near Boise. He became very home-sick for his family and hid in some grapevines so no one could see him cry. As he grew older, he spent many enjoyable summers at the ranch. There he helped to milk the cows, feed the chickens and gather eggs, pick berries, and do other chores. Sometimes he and his cousins drove a horse and buggy to a small town nearby. There they earned money by selling the farm products door-to-door.

After they finished their chores, Howard and the children found lots of fun things to do. They could ride horses, hike to a river, fish in a pond, go swimming, or play games. At night they sometimes slept on top of a haystack and watched the stars and moon in the black sky.

When Howard started school, he worried that his teacher might find out he was color blind. He learned a clever way to deal with this problem. He lined up his crayons in a row on his desk. Any time the teacher told the students to pick up a certain color, he would run his hand over the top of the crayons. When his hand touched the crayon the teacher asked them to use, the little girl behind him would tap him on the shoulder. Howard was happy when Dorothy started school two years later. They could then walk together to school, which was one mile from their home.

After school and on Saturdays Howard liked to go down to the river near his home to fish, swim, watch the beavers and birds, and sail toy boats. He and Dorothy also played together and took care of each other. Once some neighborhood bullies kept taking Howard's cap and putting it on some railroad tracks so it would be flat-tened by the trains whizzing by. After his mother com-plained that she was tired of buying him new caps, Dorothy told the boys, "If you don't lay off, I'll beat you up!"

Howard's father was a motorman on a train that ran between downtown Boise and several small towns west of the city. Howard and Dorothy liked to walk to the train stop near their home and ride with their father to the neighboring towns and back again.

When Howard and Dorothy were little, their parents read to them in the evenings. Their father was well read, and one of their favorite games was to sit on the floor at his feet and hear him ask, "Where shall we travel today?" Using an atlas and encyclopedias, they would learn about the United States and other countries.

Later the children got their own library cards. Dorothy's favorite books were the Pollyanna series. She also liked to read the books of James Fenimore Cooper and Louisa May Alcott. Howard's favorite books were *Tom Sawyer, Huckleberry Finn,* and the Tom Swift series.

From the time he was very young, Howard helped his parents around the house. He learned to polish the letters on the coal stove in the kitchen, chop wood, bring buckets of coal from an outside shed into the house, scatter grain for the chickens, take fresh water to the rabbits and other animals in the backyard, weed the vegetable garden, and cut the lawn. Howard was also known for his mechanical abilities. If he found an old alarm clock that had been thrown away, he would repair it and then sell it. Later, when he owned a car, if it needed to be repaired he would sometimes make the car parts himself with his tools.

Every evening Howard walked half a mile to get fresh milk for his family from a farmer who had cows. He often brought milk back for the widows who lived on their lane. He would also mow their lawns, and if they could not pay him, he would do it anyway because he liked to help people.

On Howard's eleventh birthday, he received fifty cents and a playful birthday spanking from his mother, fifty cents from his father, and a pair of gloves from Dorothy. She and five of her friends had organized a sewing club. When they met at the Hunter home that day, they ran after Howard, and each of them gave him a birthday spanking. Then they all played games and sang songs. Later that day Howard and Dorothy played the new piano their parents had bought for them two weeks earlier, on Dorothy's birthday. Howard took piano lessons for just a few months. However, he really enjoyed music and taught himself to play by ear.

When Howard and Dorothy were young, the Hunters did not have an automobile. They went downtown on the streetcar and traveled by train when they visited family members in neighboring towns. The children were excited when their father finally bought an automobile, a Hupmobile, and took them on a vacation to a mountain resort 120 miles north of Boise. When they arrived, one of the rear wheels of the car broke through a weak place in the road and into a pool of boiling-hot water from an underground spring. Howard's father broke off a pole from a fence and used it as a lever to lift the car out of the pool before the tire melted. The family then enjoyed their vacation, which included swimming in the warm springs and hiking in the hills.

Howard's mother was active in the Boise Branch of The Church of Jesus Christ of Latter-day Saints. His father was not a member of the Church, but he supported his wife and children in their church activities. When Howard turned eight years old, he wanted to be baptized, but his father explained that he wanted him to wait until he grew up so he could decide for himself which church to join. Two years later, when Dorothy turned eight, she too was told that she would have to wait to be baptized.

When Howard turned twelve, he begged his father to let him be baptized so he could become a deacon. The other boys his age were deacons and were able to pass the sacrament, get the building ready for Sunday School, pump the bellows for the organ, and cut kindling for the wood stove that heated the room the members met in. Finally, a few months after Howard's twelfth birthday, his father agreed to let him and Dorothy be baptized.

They were baptized in a big public swimming pool, since the Church had no baptismal font in Boise at that time.

Now that he was a member of the Church, Howard also joined the Boy Scout troop sponsored by the Boise Branch. Three years later, when he was fifteen, he became the second Scout in Boise to receive his Eagle. He had earned thirty-two badges.

In high school he took shop classes and developed his woodworking skills. He was a member of an army training group, the Reserve Officers Training Corps, and became a major, the highest rank in the organization. He also won several awards for his ability to handle a rifle. From the time he was a young boy, he always worked to earn money for the things he wanted. Among his after-school and summer jobs were golf caddie, assistant to a pharmacist, advertising writer for a newspaper, hotel bellboy, and janitor in an art supply store.

Though he had no formal music training except for a few piano and violin lessons, Howard taught himself to play the drums, clarinet, trumpet, saxophone, and marimba. When he was seventeen, he organized a five-piece orchestra to play at dances and other social events. The group was called Hunter's Croonaders. After he graduated from high school, he and the other musicians signed a contract with a cruise ship that was sailing across the Pacific Ocean to the Orient. They played music on the ship for dinners and dances and even provided background music for the silent movies shown in the ship's theater.

When Howard returned home ten weeks later, his father surprised him with the news that he had been baptized while Howard was on the cruise!

A few months after he returned home, Howard W. Hunter moved to Los Angeles, California. There he went to work at a bank and got married. Then he decided to go back to school to get a law degree. He worked all day and took classes at night for four years and graduated with honors from law school in 1939.

Two years later he was called to serve as a bishop. The young people of his ward knew that their bishop loved them very much, but he could also be firm in his dealings with them. One Sunday after they had passed the sacrament, some of the Aaronic Priesthood boys slipped out of church and went to a soda fountain next door to have malted milk drinks. Bishop Hunter left the meeting and followed them. "Brethren," he said as he entered the malt shop, "when you have finished your malts, we will continue our meeting." The boys gulped their drinks down very quickly and followed him back to the chapel.

Howard W. Hunter was called to the Council of the Twelve Apostles in October 1959. As an apostle, he organized many new stakes and dedicated Panama and Austria for the preaching of the gospel. He served as head of the Family History Department and was in charge of building the Brigham Young University Center in Jerusalem. He also directed a major expansion of the Polynesian Cultural Center in Hawaii. As a leader, he inspired great confidence in those he met and worked with.

On June 5, 1994, Howard W. Hunter became the fourteenth president of the Church. Despite severe physical ailments, he visited the Saints in many areas of the world and dedicated new temples in Orlando, Florida, and Bountiful, Utah.

President Hunter was known as a gentle and kind man. He taught the Saints to live more Christlike lives and to attend the temple more often. He died on March 3, 1995. He served as prophet for just nine months, the shortest time of any prophet in the latter-day Church.

GORDON   B.

HINCKLEY

Six-year-old Gordon and his four-and-a-half-year-old brother, Sherman, were asleep in the seats of their dad's Model T Ford. That much was not unusual. They were used to sleeping under the stars at their summer farmhouse in the country. But this time they were on a family vacation. Their parents had decided to go to Yellowstone Park with their brand-new car during the summer of 1916. Pulling off to the side of the road, they set up camp. Sometime in the night a big bear came out of the forest and began sniffing all around the car. The noise of its claws scratching as it tried to stand up against the car woke up their father in the tent nearby. When he saw the bear, he immediately lit a fire to scare it away. Before the bear left, it had been close enough to the sleeping boys in the car to lick little brother Sherman's forehead!

Gordon B. Hinckley was born June 23, 1910. He was the first child born to Ada and Bryant Hinckley, but he was not the only child in the household. His father's first wife, Christine, had died, leaving eight children. Bryant then married Ada Bitner, a teacher from the LDS Business College, and she did her best to help the children who had lost their mother. Being a teacher, she was used to being around young people, and she brought the two families together so well that they never thought of themselves as being "Christine's children" or "Ada's children." They were the Hinckley children.

Gordon's family lived in downtown Salt Lake City. His mother had her baby grand piano in the parlor. Both his mother and father collected books. Together they created a library in one room of the house with more than a thousand books. Gordon's mother had collected elegant china, crystal glasses, silverware, and linens. She was a skilled hostess and taught her children how to entertain guests.

As a child, Gordon had lots of earaches, allergies, asthma, and hay fever. When he was two years old, he got whooping cough. That made him very weak and sickly. Because the soot from everyone's coal stoves and furnaces hung in the city air, it was hard for Gordon to breathe. The doctor said he needed some fresh, clean, country air before he could get better. So his parents bought five acres of farmland by Millcreek Canyon and built a summer home there.

Their three-bedroom country farmhouse did not have many of the nice things their city home had. It had no electricity or plumbing. They used kerosene lamps for light. Spring water had to be carried into the house, and they used an outhouse for their bathroom. But the Hinckleys all loved their country home!

Gordon's best friend was his younger brother, Sherman. They were born only a year and a half apart. Sherman was healthier than Gordon and grew tall, so they looked almost the same age. Each summer the Hinckley family stayed at their country home, and Gordon's coughing went away. The boys had a list of chores each day to be done by noon, and the rest of the day was theirs to play. They ran through the fields barefoot all summer. They explored the gullies around the farm and up the canyon and went swimming every day.

In between weeding, feeding chickens and other farm animals, gathering eggs, irrigating the garden, pruning the fruit trees, and milking the cows, Gordon and Sherman learned to shoot targets with .22 rifles, listened to their mother's classical music on the old record player, played games, and developed strong mechanical talents. Over the years the two boys built home appliances, fixed the Model T Ford and other cars, made toys for their sisters, and learned enough chemistry to build explosives to loosen dirt that was too hard to plow.

The Hinckley family spent each winter in their city home. Shoveling coal, washing dishes, and emptying the dripper pan under the icebox were some of the winter chores. Spring and fall housecleaning always meant beating the carpets on the clothesline, cleaning the wallpaper, and washing the windows. The boys liked Saturdays. Their dad worked at the Deseret Gym, and they could go there with him to swim and play sports.

When Gordon was five years old, the prophet, President Joseph F. Smith, announced that all families were to have a weekly family night. At first it was awkward because the children felt self-conscious about speaking or singing in front of each other. They giggled a lot instead. But, after a while, it became easier. In fact, most family nights became good ones and made the family members feel very close to each other.

When Gordon turned six years old it was time to go to school, but Gordon did not want to go. He did not want to wear the school uniforms with shirt, tie, short pants, long stockings, and shoes after being barefoot and free all summer. His parents decided that, because he was small for his age, he could wait to go to school until the next year.

The next year Gordon was seven. He still did not like the idea of school and a school uniform. He started school with his younger brother, Sherman, crying the whole way. But Gordon was so smart that he soon caught up to his own age group and attended with them.

All of the Hinckley children were known for their good manners, good eating habits, good posture, good social skills, and good communication skills. Their mother insisted that they use perfect grammar in speaking and writing. Every evening they read from the scriptures or listened to their parents read stories to them.

One day when Gordon was about seven or eight years old, he was sitting on the front porch with some of his friends. His mother overheard him saying unkind things about a family who was walking down the street. She immediately took Gordon and his friends into the living room and scolded them. When corrected by his parents, Gordon obeyed.

Gordon and Sherman were together so much that there came a time when they began to fight over everything. One day their father brought home boxing gloves for them and told them to "get it resolved once and for all." They did. And they have remained good friends ever since!

The year Gordon turned eleven, he received his patriarchal blessing. Despite his health problems and small size, he was told, in part, "Thou shalt grow to the full stature of manhood and shall become a mighty and valiant leader in the midst of Israel. . . . The nations of the earth shall hear thy voice and be brought to a knowledge of the truth." At the time, he thought that meant he would be a missionary.

When Gordon turned twelve years old, he became a Boy Scout and a deacon. One night his father took Gordon to a stake priesthood meeting. Almost four hundred men were there, and as they sang "Praise to the Man," a song about the Prophet Joseph Smith, a new feeling came over Gordon. It was a feeling the boy had never had before. Later he wrote about this experience, "I felt a great moving power, both emotional and spiritual. . . . There came into my heart a conviction . . . by the power of the Holy Ghost, that Joseph Smith was indeed a prophet of God." This new feeling and knowledge stayed with Gordon and helped him through many trials.

When Gordon entered seventh grade, the new school building he and his classmates were supposed to move into was too crowded. They were told they would have to stay at the elementary school for their seventh-grade year. Some of the boys, including Gordon, were upset by this news and decided to "show them a lesson" by not going to school at all. The next day the principal told all of them they had to have a note from their parents to get back into school. Gordon was embarrassed to ask for the note. However, his mother wrote it, asking the principal to excuse her son's "impulse to follow the crowd." His mother's words hurt him, and he decided then and there never to follow the crowd again on any decisions. He also found out that it was not the building but the teachers that were important for learning at school.

On another seventh-grade occasion, Gordon came home from a hard day at school and said a swearword. His mother immediately washed out his mouth with soap, and he never did it again!

In 1925, at age fifteen, Gordon began attending LDS High School. Church standards were expected of the staff and students, just like at the Brigham Young Academy in Provo, because the school was owned by the LDS Church. Gordon's whole attitude toward school changed, and he was excited to go. He said, "There was great morale and rapport among the student body—a tremendous spirit." Because Gordon could feel the Spirit of the Holy Ghost at this school, he felt free to be himself and progress as a child of God should.

Gordon went on to the University of Utah and was able to go on a mission to England after he graduated. While in England, Gordon became sick with allergies again. Although he soon overcame his fear of speaking in the town square, he and the other missionaries didn't find many people who were interested in hearing the gospel lessons. One day he wrote to his father that he felt he was wasting his time and his father's money.

Several mornings later, during their scripture study time, Gordon and his companion read Mark 8:35, "For whosoever will save his life shall lose it; but whosoever shall lose his life for my sake and the gospel's, the same shall save it." Later that same day he got a letter from his father. It said, "Dear Gordon, I have your recent letter. I have only one suggestion: forget yourself and go to work. Love, Dad." Gordon went to the bedroom and prayed. He promised that he would try to forget his own problems and lose himself in serving Heavenly Father. "That July day in 1933 was my day of decision," he remembered later. "Everything good that has happened to me since then I can trace back to the decision I made that day."

Gordon B. Hinckley was called to be an apostle in 1961, and he was later a counselor to three Church presidents: Spencer W. Kimball, Ezra Taft Benson, and Howard W. Hunter. On March 12, 1995, President Hinckley was ordained as the fifteenth prophet of The Church of Jesus Christ of Latter-day Saints. When a reporter asked for the theme of his presidency, he answered, "Carry on. Yes. Our theme will be to carry on the great work which has been furthered by our predecessors."

And carry on he has! President Hinckley has expressed his and Heavenly Father's love for the Saints, missionaries, and youth all over the world. He has been interviewed by television and newspaper reporters in many different countries. In February 1996, he announced that there were more Latter-day Saints living outside of the United States than inside, with a total Church membership of ten million in about 160 nations.

His repeated counsel is to "Keep trying. Be believing. Be happy. Don't get discouraged. Things will work out." One can easily see how President Gordon B. Hinckley has been protected, prepared, and polished to be the prophet at this important time in the history of the Church and of the world.

BIBLIOGRAPHY

Backman, Milton V. *Joseph Smith's First Vision: The First Vision in Its Historical Context.* Salt Lake City: Bookcraft, 1971.

Barrett, Ivan J. *Joseph Smith and the Restoration.* 3rd edition. Provo, Utah: Brigham Young University Press, 1970.

"Church Coming Out of Obscurity." *Church News,* 30 August 1997.

Church of Jesus Christ of Latter-day Saints, The. *Targeteer B Lesson Manual.* Primary Association.

Church of Jesus Christ of Latter-day Saints, The. *Course 13/14 Sunday School Lesson Manual.*

Cornwall, Rebecca, and Richard F. Palmer. "The Religious and Family Background of Brigham Young." *BYU Studies,* Spring 1978, 286–310.

Cowley, Matthias F. *Wilford Woodruff: History of His Life and Labors as Recorded in His Daily Journals.* Salt Lake City: Bookcraft, 1964.

Dew, Sheri L. *Ezra Taft Benson, A Biography.* Salt Lake City: Deseret Book, 1987.

———. *Go Forward with Faith: The Biography of Gordon B. Hinckley.* Salt Lake City: Deseret Book, 1996.

Faust, James E. "Howard W. Hunter: Man of God." *Ensign,* April 1995.

———. "The Way of an Eagle." *Ensign,* August 1994.

"Gordon B. Hinckley, An Anchor of Faith." *Ensign,* September 1994.

"Gordon B. Hinckley, Man of Integrity, 15th President." video cassette. Salt Lake City: The Church of Jesus Christ of Latter-day Saints, 1995.

Hartley, William G. "Ezra Taft Benson." In *Presidents of the Church,* 3rd edition, edited by Leonard J. Arrington. Salt Lake City: Deseret Book, 1989.

Hartshorn, Leon R., compiler. *Classic Stories from the Lives of Our Prophets.* Salt Lake City: Deseret Book, 1971.

Hinckley, Bryant S. *Heber J. Grant: Highlights in the Life of a Great Leader.* Salt Lake City: Deseret Book, 1959.

Hinckley, Gordon B. "Some Lessons I Learned as a Boy." *Ensign,* May 1993.

Holland, Jeffrey R. "President Gordon B. Hinckley, Stalwart and Brave He Stands." *Ensign,* June 1995.

Howard W. Hunter, Prophet of God. video cassette. Salt Lake City: The Church of Jesus Christ of Latter-day Saints, 1994.

Jessee, Dean C. "Brigham Young's Family." *BYU Studies,* Spring 1978, 311–27.

Kimball, Edward L., and Andrew E. Kimball, Jr. *Spencer W. Kimball.* Salt Lake City: Bookcraft, 1977.

Knowles, Eleanor. *Howard W. Hunter.* Salt Lake City: Deseret Book, 1994.

Leavitt, Melvin. "A Boy from Whitney." *New Era,* November 1986.

McCune, George M. *Gordon B. Hinckley, Shoulder for the Lord.* Salt Lake City: Hawkes Publishing, 1996.

McKay, Llewelyn R. *Home Memories of President David O. McKay.* Salt Lake City: Deseret Book, 1971.

"Milestones in a Life of Service: President Howard W. Hunter." *Ensign,* April 1995.

"Modern-day Trek." *Ensign,* July 1997.

Monson, Thomas S. "President Howard W. Hunter: A Man for All Seasons." *Ensign,* April 1995.

Morrell, Jeanette McKay. *Highlights in the Life of President David O. McKay.* Salt Lake City: Deseret Book, 1971.

"Music Filled Early Years with Harmony." *Deseret News,* 4 March 1995.

Neeley, Deta Peterson, and Nathan Glen Neeley. *A Child's Story of the Prophet Joseph Smith.* Salt Lake City: Deseret News Press, 1958.

———. *A Child's Story of the Prophet Brigham Young.* Salt Lake City: Deseret News Press, 1959.

————. *A Child's Story of the Prophet John Taylor*. Salt Lake City: Deseret News Press, 1960.

————. *A Child's Story of the Prophet Wilford Woodruff*. Salt Lake City: Deseret News Press, 1962.

————. *A Child's Story of the Prophet Lorenzo Snow*. Salt Lake City: Deseret Book, 1968.

Nibley, Preston. *Joseph Smith the Prophet*. Salt Lake City: Deseret News Press, 1946.

Payne, Jaynann Morgan. "Louisa Bingham Lee: Sacrifice and Spirit." *Ensign*, February 1974.

"Pres. Hunter, 87, After a Life Giving Service." *Deseret News*, 3 March 1995.

"President Ezra Taft Benson Still Strong at Ninety!" *Ensign*, August 1989.

Ricks, Kellene. "Ezra Taft Benson." *Friend*, January 1990.

Romney, Thomas C. *The Life of Lorenzo Snow, Fifth President of The Church of Jesus Christ of Latter-day Saints*. Salt Lake City: Sons of Utah Pioneers Memorial Foundation, 1955.

Smith, Joseph Fielding. *The Life of Joseph F. Smith, Sixth President of The Church of Jesus Christ of Latter-day Saints*. Salt Lake City: Deseret Book, 1969.

Smith, Joseph Fielding, Jr., and John J. Stewart. *The Life of Joseph Fielding Smith, Tenth President of The Church of Jesus Christ of Latter-day Saints*. Salt Lake City: Deseret Book, 1972.

Smith, Lucy Mack. *History of Joseph Smith by His Mother Lucy Mack Smith*, with notes and comments by Preston Nibley. Salt Lake City: Bookcraft, 1958.

Snow, Eliza R. *Biography and Family Record of Lorenzo Snow*. Salt Lake City: Deseret News Company Printers, 1884.

"Sweet Is the Work, Gordon B. Hinckley, 15th President of the Church." *New Era*, May 1995.

Van Orden, Dell. "Remembrances of Past Birthdays." *Church News*, 4 August 1990.

"Viewpoint, Prophet of the Lord." *Church News*, 8 April 1995.

West, Emerson Roy. *Profiles of the Presidents.* 1st edition. Salt Lake City: Deseret Book, 1972.

Wirthlin, Joseph B. "Living Water to Quench Spiritual Thirst." *Ensign,* May 1995.

Young, S. Dilworth. *Young Brigham Young.* Salt Lake City: Bookcraft, 1962.